Software Engineering Approaches to Enable Digital Transformation Technologies

Software Engineering Approaches to Enable Digital Transformation Technologies features contributions reflecting ideas and research in enabling digital transformation technologies through software engineering. To date, multiple, different approaches have been adopted to develop software solutions for a variety of different problems. Of all the available approaches, the main approaches are level-oriented, data flow-oriented, data structure-oriented, and object-oriented design approaches. The other focus of the book is digital transformation, which can be defined as the adoption of digital technology to improve efficiency, value, and innovation.

Digitalization is more than just putting additional technological systems and services in place. Rather than improving conventional methods, a true digital transformation initiative includes radically rethinking company structures and procedures. There are four types of digital transformation: business process, business model, domain, and cultural and organizational. Companies are being challenged to develop new business models that consider and harness digitalization. From the standpoint of software engineering, digital transformation alters how software is built.

Current trends include the development of mobile applications, cloud applications, and Internet of Things (IoT) applications. Emerging trends are the development of digital twins, robotics, artificial intelligence, machine learning, augmented reality, and additive manufacturing. This book examines the challenges that arise due to digitization in society and presents plausible solutions that could be applied to counter these challenges and convert them into opportunities. These solutions may further be improvised and worked out for the software companies from the technological perspective, organizational perspective, and management perspective.

Prof. Sanjay Misra, PhD, is a scientist at the Department of Applied Data Science, Institute of Energy Technology, Halden, Norway. He is also a senior member of the Institute of Electrical and Electronics Engineers (IEEE).

Amit Jain, PhD, MBA, FDP, is vice chancellor, dean of the Faculty of Management Studies, and director of Amity Business School, Amity University, India.

Manju Kaushik, PhD, MCA, MTech CS, MSc, MBA, is a professor, Amity Institute of Information Technology, and the president of the Institute's Innovation Council, Amity University Rajasthan, India.

Prof. Chitresh Banerjee, PhD, MTech CS, MCA, B.Sc., GNIIT, is an associate professor, Amity Institute of Information Technology, and the vice president of the Institute's Innovation Council, Amity University Rajasthan, India. He is also a member of Machine Intelligence Research (MIR) Labs, United States.

Software Engineering Approaches to Enable Digital Transformation Technologies

Edited by Sanjay Misra,
Amit Jain, Manju Kaushik,
and Chitresh Banerjee

Routledge
Taylor & Francis Group

LONDON AND NEW YORK

First edition published 2024
by Routledge
4 Park Square, Milton Park, Abingdon, Oxon OX14 4RN

and by Routledge
605 Third Avenue, New York, NY 10158

Routledge is an imprint of the Taylor & Francis Group, an informa business

© 2024 Routledge

ISBN: 9781032571300 (hbk)
ISBN: 9781032579214 (pbk)
ISBN: 9781003441601 (ebk)

DOI: 10.1201/9781003441601

Typeset in Garamond
by Apex CoVantage, LLC

Contents

12 Emerging and Growing Technologies in Blockchain Security: A Review

VIDIT KESARWANI, HONEY GOCHER, AMIT K SINGH, AND
YUDHVEER SINGH

Preface

Software Engineering Approaches to Enable Digital Transformation Technologies covers contributions reflecting ideas and research in enabling digital transformation technologies using software engineering approaches. So far, different approaches have been adopted to develop software solutions for a variety of different problems. Of all the available approaches, the main approaches are the level-oriented, data flow-oriented, data structure-oriented, and object-oriented design approaches. The development approach is described as a series of crises that the process goes through as it grows and evolves. Each of these crises is the result of a conflict between the old self and the new abilities and attitudes that are constantly developing and expanding. Digital transformation can be defined as the adoption of technology which is digital in nature to improve efficiency, value, and innovation. In other words, we can say that the process of employing digital technology to build new or adapt current business processes, culture, and customer experiences to satisfy changing business and market requirements is known as digital transformation.

Digitalization is more than just putting additional technological systems and services in place. Rather than fiddling with or improving conventional methods, a true digital transformation initiative includes radically rethinking company structures and procedures. There are four types of digital transformation: business process, business model, domain, and cultural/organizational. Companies are being challenged to change, i.e., to develop new business models that consider and harness rising digitalization. As a result, from the standpoint of software engineering, digital transformation alters how software is built. Some current trends are the development of mobile applications, cloud applications, and Internet of Things (IoT) applications. Some emerging trends are the development of digital twins, robotics, artificial intelligence, machine learning, augmented reality, additive manufacturing, etc. The proposed book examines the challenges that arise due to digitization in society and some of the plausible solutions and support which could be applied to counter these challenges and convert them into opportunities. These solutions may further be improvised and worked out for the software companies from the technological perspective, organizational perspective, and management perspective.

The topics covered in this special issue include precise prediction of water level using the Naïve Bayes algorithm for smart irrigation in pomegranate farms, a brief review on lightweight practice of docker vulnerabilities, deep learning-based serverless image handler using Amazon web services, ontology-based delegation enforcement in the cloud ecosystem, the applicability of artificial intelligence for social development in rural and urban sectors, disease prediction using Bayes' theorem, a secure voting system using blockchain technology, deployment of a new life cycle model for applications of the web, the future possibilities of artificial intelligence in modern drapes, mobile application, communication, and ant colony optimization re-sampling: enhancing the performance of imbalanced classification. It is hoped that *Software Engineering Approaches to Enable Digital Transformation Technologies* will make a good reference material and be of great use for researchers, academicians, and industry professionals working in the related field.

Sanjay Misra,
Østfold University College,
Halden, Norway

Amit Jain, Manju Kaushik, Chitresh Banerjee
Amity University
Rajasthan, Jaipur, India

Contributors

Ayush Pritam Bage
Amity Institute of Information Technology
Amity University Rajasthan
Jaipur, Rajasthan, India

Barkha Bahl
Department of Computer Science
Trinity Institute of Professional Studies
Delhi, India

Parul Dubey
Department of Information Technology
Shri Shankaracharya Institute of
   Professional Management and
   Technology
Raipur, Chhattisgarh, India

Pushkar Dubey
Department of Management
Pandit Sundarlal Sharma (Open)
   University
Bilaspur, Chhattisgarh, India

Honey Gocher
Amity Institute of Information
   Technology
Amity University Rajasthan
Jaipur, Rajasthan, India

Dimpy Jindal
Department of Computer Science
Delhi Institute of Advanced Studies
Delhi, India

Anuj Kalwar
Department of Computer Science and
   Engineering
JECRC University
Jaipur, Rajasthan, India

Ishwinder Kaur
Amity Institute of Fashion
   Technology
Amity University Rajasthan
Jaipur, Rajasthan, India

Manju Kaushik
Amity Institute of Information
   Technology
Amity University Rajasthan
Jaipur, Rajasthan, India

Vidit Kesarwani
ACPL
Gurugram, Haryana, India

Satendra Kumar
Department of Computer Science and
   Engineering
MIT
Moradabad, U.P., India

Sushil Kumar
Amity Institute of Information
   Technology
Amity University Rajasthan
Jaipur, Rajasthan, India

S. Neduncheliyan
Department of Computer Science and
    Engineering
Bharath University
Chennai, Tamil Nadu, India

Nikita Patil
IT Department
Adani Enterprises Ltd.
Ahmedabad, Gujarat, India

Reeti Raj
Department of Sociology & Social Work
Banasthali Vidyapith
Banasthali, Rajasthan, India

Sambaditya Raj
Amity Institute of Fashion Technology
Amity University Rajasthan
Jaipur, Rajasthan, India

Shalu J. Rajawat
IT Department
Genpact Inc.
Gurugram, Haryana, India

Kailash Kumar Sahu
Department of Management
Pandit Sundarlal Sharma (Open)
    University
Bilaspur, Chhattisgarh, India

Sameer Saxena
Amity Institute of Information
    Technology
Amity University Rajasthan
Jaipur, Rajasthan, India

Deepika Shekhawat
Department of Computer Science and
    Engineering
Manipal University
Jaipur, Rajasthan, India

Amit Kumar Singh
Amity Institute of Information
    Technology
Amity University Rajasthan
Jaipur, Rajasthan, India

Yudhveer Singh
Amity Institute of Information
    Technology
Amity University Rajasthan
Jaipur, Rajasthan, India

Swapnali Tandel
Department of Computer Science
Nagindas Khandwala College
Malad, Maharastra, India

Kshitij Thakur
AISSMS
IOIT
Pune, Maharashtra, India

Pragya Vaishnav
Department of Computer Science
Nagindas Khandwala College
Malad, Maharastra, India

Viplesh
IT Department, C-DAC
Noida, Uttar Pradesh, India

Prashant B. Wakhare
Department of Computer Science and
    Engineering
Bharath University
Chennai, Tamil Nadu, India

Surendra Kumar Yadav
Department of Computer Science and
    Engineering
Poornima College of Engineering
Jaipur, Rajasthan, India

Chapter 1

Precise Prediction of Water Level Using the Naïve Bayes Algorithm for Smart Irrigation in Pomegranate Farms

Prashant B. Wakhare,
S. Neduncheliyan, and Kshitij Thakur

1.1 Introduction

Firstly, the discussion is focused on the comparison between cereals and fruits. The following paragraph explains advantages of horticulture over cereal cultivation. Seventy per cent of the world's small scale intensive agriculture is practiced in China and India, with China holding 193 million (47%) and India holding 93 million (23%) small farms respectively. It has been estimated in a study that by 2050 around 93% of agriculture will fall under this category in India. Therefore it becomes necessary for the agricultural producers of the nation to provide international quality standards produce with less stress being imposed on environment [1]. With operational farm holdings in India being less than one hectare, and with emphasis given to cereal production, there is a high risk of crop losses due to biotic and abiotic stresses. Also these crops consume a lot of water, and according to the Food Corporation of India, the nation has an excess of cereals with

DOI: 10.1201/9781003441601-1

1

no storage spaces. This indicates that large amounts of natural resources are wasted in producing excess cereals. Drought zone is increasing day by day and making all agriculture sectors more challenging in all aspects. On the other hand horticulture requires less water and provides higher returns. Hence, it is necessary to make use of available technologies and increase the land under cultivation to horticulture. It is mostly seen that small farmers are having to combine water resources such as wells, bore wells, join pipelines from nearby water resource, etc. Thereby one cannot also neglect water management. Focus on this aspect of agriculture can save the farmers from natural calamities and crisis.

One such fruit taken under horticulture is pomegranate (Figure 1.1). The pomegranate (*Punica granatum*) is grown in tropical and subtropical regions of the world. The total area under cultivation of pomegranate in India is 107,000 ha and production is around 743,000 thousand tons [2]. Maharashtra is the leading producer of pomegranates followed by Karnataka, Andhra Pradesh, Gujarat, and Tamil Nadu. **Ganesh**, **Bhagwa**, **Ruby**, **Arakta**, and **Mridula** are the different varieties of pomegranates produced in Maharashtra. In India, pomegranate is commercially cultivated in the Solapur, Sangli, Nasik, Ahmednagar, Pune, Dhule, Aurangabad, Satara, Osmanabad, and Latur districts of Maharashtra; the Bijapur, Belgaum, and Bagalkot districts of Karnataka; and to a smaller extent in Gujarat, Andhra Pradesh, and Tamil Nadu. Pomegranate cultivation can have a huge impact on its yield based on the watering pattern and seasonal changes in climate which is further proved in the following study. Considering the aforementioned factors that may affect the yield, we are providing a system which can bring the best yield using precise water availability. During the summer period of the Indian subcontinent, water availability is at all-time low. This number is hitting much lower counts year by year. Hence the pomegranate orchards are affected badly due to lack of irrigation

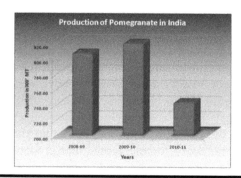

Figure 1.1 Pomegranate production in India.

Source: Agri-exchange magazine by APEDA and United Nations Conference on Trade and Development on Pomegranate http://apeda.in/agriexchange/ Market%20Profile/one/POMEGRANATE.aspx

facility during this period. This may lead to heavy losses for the orchard managers and farmers [3–5].

According to the data published by **National Horticulture Board of India** there is a gradual decline in the area of pomegranate cultivation in India from 109,000 ha in 2008–09 to 107,000 ha in 2010–11; similarly, the production has decreased from 807,000 tons to 743,000 tons during the same period.

This is also supported by a report by the *Indian Express* that drought and water scarcity have added to the pain of farmers and will affect the yield by 25% [6].

1.2 Literature Survey

Now considering the aforementioned problems it is quite clear that a solution is the need of the hour. A lot of study has been dedicated regarding technology-assisted agriculture. Implementation of the Internet of Things and machine learning has been widely promoted in these studies [7]. Malche T. in the research study has proposed a prototyping system in order to monitor the water management of a water resource using the Internet of Things (IoT). This study focuses on the precise usage of the available water and monitors the levels over the air. However the research was limited only to prototype level. The IoT architecture is developed around Ethernet shield which is not advisable for large farms. Apart from this, Ethernet implementation increases cost and maintenance charges, thereby making the system infeasible.

The IoT does not limit only to the ground operations [8]. Making use of unmanned aerial vehicles (UAV) applications of precision farming can scale heights. Making use of UAV drones carrying high-precision sensors can enable real-time monitoring. With this application huge grounds can be covered aerially and data can be collected. Further, this data collected can be analyzed to make decisions for further operations on crops. However, there is still a lot of time for the rural population to get accustomed to such UAVs [9]. Further in this discussion it is important to understand the slope of the focused area. This problem has also been stated in the study carried out by Choi. In this study, the authors have provided an excellent algorithm called the random forest to measure the water level of the sources. They have considered other factors such as temperature, precipitation, etc. However they have highlighted the need to understand the backflow which may happen during rainy season. R. Nageswara Rao [10] has given an IOT-based smart crop field monitoring and automation irrigation system. This system optimizes the uses of water fertilizers while maximizing the yield of the crops and also will help in analyzing the weather condition of the field. However, the authors have not discussed the magnitude by which there will be an increase in the quality and quantity of the yield. S. M. Kamruzzaman [11] has produced a chapter called "Promoting Greenness with IoT-Based Plant Growth System." This chapter has given new IoT-based technology, which brings device interoperability and machine-to-machine operations to unprecedented levels. Along with the website there is also an Android application so as to increase the accessibility of the users. Joaquin Gutierrez [12] has proposed an automated irrigation system using a wireless sensor network and GPRS module. This irrigation system allowed cultivation in places with water scarcity thereby improving sustainability. Besides the monitory saving in water use, the importance of the preservation of these natural resources justified the use of this kind of irrigation system. The authors have developed systems only for small areas. Therefore the scalability comes under question while implementing on large scale. Nurzaman Ahmed [13] has proposed an Internet of Things (IoT) for smart precision agriculture and farming in rural areas, where network latency is reduced to a certain extent. In this, a cross layer-based channel access and routing solutions for sensing and actuating is proposed. The authors have discussed only an Internet point of view. They have not commented in detail regarding the implementation and methodology to develop the system in benefit of the farmer. Nikesh Gondchawar [14] has proposed IoT-based smart agriculture. It helped to improve the yields of the crop and overall production by using a smart irrigation system. The authors have used old technology.

1.3 Methodology

The pomegranate plant is very sensitive towards the irrigation patterns being implemented [15, 16]. Less or excess watering leads to damage of the whole fruit season. So precise watering is must. Today we are using a drip irrigation system which can be controlled acre-wise. Now, we are proposing a system wherein the monitoring will shift from acre-wise to the individual plant. In drip irrigation there is a major pipe at a column and then it gets divided into small pipes in rows. At each row we are providing a main valve and servomotor attached to it. Then at existing drip irrigation there is a nozzle at every plant. We are proposing an IT-based solution to automate the nozzle operation at every plant location. The roots of the plants are the source absorbents. The moisture in the soil passes through into the roots through the process of osmosis. Hence it is important to keep a check on the moisture content of the soil. This is monitored by a series of nodes of moisture sensors installed near each plant at a depth of 70–80 cm. This height is approximately close to the root penetration of the plants. These sensors will relay the real-time data to our controller, from where it will be passed over the air for further processing. This is followed by the main phase of our solution. We then will process the data to understand the water requirements of the plant. On the basis of this data and analysis further actions will be taken keeping in mind the available amount of water. But this method can become too elaborative if every time the whole process needs to be executed on the basis of real-time data. However if this dataset generated in the initial phase can be trained in such a manner so as to understand the habits of the plant, the whole water requirement can be predicted for the complete cycle of flowering (Figure 1.2).

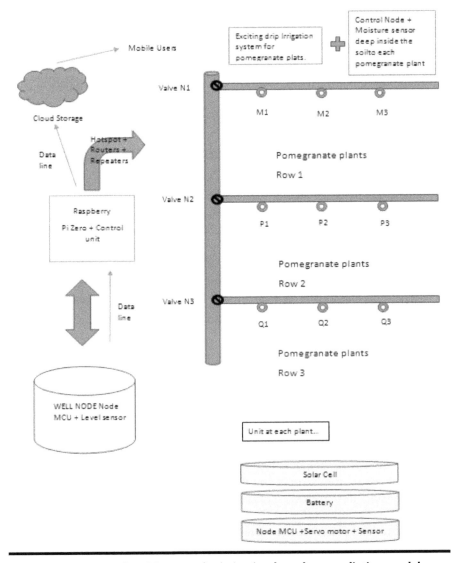

Figure 1.2   Proposed architecture for irrigation based on prediction model.

Our design of an artificial intelligence algorithm will map the patterns of soil moisture content of the individual plants and create a prediction report for the requirements. This mapping of requirements will then be compared to a previously trained dataset and accordingly on the basis of prediction report watering will be executed. This will help the farmers to prepare beforehand for any shortcomings such as less or excessive rains and avoid unpredictable damages. The

AI-controlled irrigation facility will further add to the yield of the crops. Thus over time the AI machine will become more efficient in analyzing the plants' requirements and generating reports for future [17]. We are using the Naïve Bayes algorithm as a base. This algorithm is important to consider as according to its definition, the qualities it includes are typically unique and unrelated to any measurements.

1.4 Adaptive Plant Requirement Prediction Algorithm

1. We will take x number of measurements and call them as previous measurements. Let us define measurements as the requirements of plants.
2. We are taking a set of measurements for an interval of time period t.
3. Depending on matching of previous and current measurements x over time period t we will make two classes: A and B.
4. Differential between A and B is based on the Naïve Bayes algorithm, by taking proportion of previous measurement x and multiplying it with portion of measurements in class A, if this no is bigger than corresponding calculation of B.
5. Calculus:

$$Posterior = Prior \times Likehood/Evidence$$

$$P(A/B) = P(B/A) \times P(A)/P(B)$$

It is also important to decide the priority for each plant while watering at individual level. To make it possible, we have provided the node MCU at each plant. A moisture sensor will provide the data to the node MCU and every node MCU will be attached to a central control unit, i.e., Raspberry Pi Zero. Routers and repeaters are provided for smooth transmission of the data. Also, a water level sensor is attached at the water source and it will provide that data to the control unit. According to the available water and plants' requirements, the decision will be made, for that algorithm is designed to select priority.

To fulfill power requirements, a solar cell and battery is provided at each plant so no need of wiring through the farm. Now, the same data can be uploaded to the cloud and can be used by the mobile user to analyze the working state of the system. Refer to the architecture: a servomotor is attached to the nozzle so that we can control the opening in precise degrees, and controlled irrigation can be achieved. Now in order to train the datasets and extract the proper dataset for the ideal result, it is necessary for the algorithm to also have in record the variations seen for different quality yields.

1.5 Observations

Per our experimental set-up, let us consider three subjects, A, B, and C, each of the age of 5 years. All three subjects belong to the Mridula variety of pomegranate. The subjects are investigated in the rain shadow regions of Western Maharashtra. The climate is usually dry all year round with annual temperatures between 12°C and 39°C. The annual rainfall in this region is below 50 cm annually. The site of investigation is 649 m above sea level [18, 19]. The annual humidity lies between 44% and 48%. The region primarily experiences hot and dry climate during the Ambe bahar flowering season of pomegranate (Tables 1.1 to 1.4). These subjects will be provided water according to the following table during the Ambe bahar flowering season:

Table 1.1 Expected End Result of Fruits Based on the Water Supply

Subject	Requirement to Supply Ratio	Quality
A	~1	Ideal
B	<1	Fruit Cracking
C	>1	Shrunk Fruit

The following watering pattern is followed over the flowering season: for Subject A

Table 1.2 Watering Pattern Data Followed for Subject A; Requirement and Supply (Litre/Month)

Time	Requirement	Moisture Supply
January	35–40	37.45
February	52–55	54.33
March	54–58	57.72
April	62–65	64.54
May	64–67	65.3
June	40–43	41.25
July	30–33	32.34
August	26–29	28.23
September	26–29	27.34
October	33–36	34.43
November	33–36	35.23
December	31–33	31.23

For Subject B

Table 1.3   Watering Pattern Data Followed for Subject B; Requirement and Supply (Litre/Month)

Time	Requirement	Moisture Supply
January	35–40	37.45
February	52–55	65.23
March	54–58	67.34
April	62–65	70.34
May	64–67	72.45
June	40–43	43.45
July	30–33	31.45
August	26–29	28.67
September	26–29	28.00
October	33–36	33.24
November	33–36	34.25
December	31–33	32.34

For Subject C

Table 1.4   Watering Pattern Data Followed for Subject C; Requirement and Supply (Litre/Month)

Time	Requirement	Moisture Supply
January	35–40	32.23
February	52–55	48.67
March	54–58	50.23
April	62–65	61.34
May	64–67	57.89
June	40–43	38.27
July	30–33	33.56
August	26–29	25.34
September	26–29	22.34
October	33–36	31.24
November	33–36	32.45
December	31–33	31.84

1.6 Result and Discussion

1.6.1 Part A for Identification of Ideal Irrigation Pattern

Subject A

The irrigation pattern followed for subject A resulted in a good yield of pomegranate. There were negligible cases of fruit cracking. The fruit weight was around 260 gm with dark red arils. The tree produced around 9.34 kg of pomegranate. This can be considered to be the ideal dataset for the development of a prediction model (Figures 1.3 and 1.4).

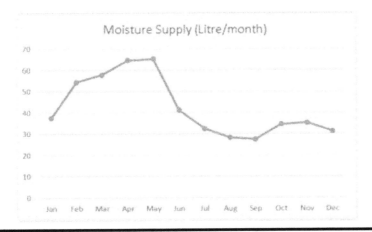

(From right) Figure 1.3   Watering pattern followed for Subject A annually based on Ambe bahar.

Figure 1.4   Requirement to supply ratio for Subject A.

Subject B

The irrigation pattern followed for Subject B resulted in 45%–50% of fruit cracking. Other healthy fruits showed ideal results. However, this irrigation method is not suggestable. This irrigation pattern falls under the <1 ratio of requirement to supply (Figures 1.5 and 1.6).

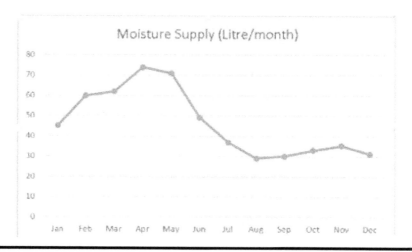

(From right) Figure 1.5   Watering pattern followed for Subject B annually based on Ambe bahar.

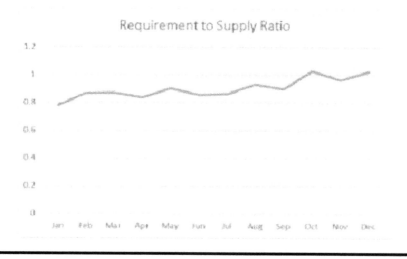

Figure 1.6   Requirement to supply ratio for Subject B.

Subject C

The irrigation pattern followed for Subject C gave below-average yield. There was a drop in the number of fruits borne by the plant. The size and weight of the plants was also below average. The percentage of fruits falling under the ideal category was around 35%. This is a water-deprived irrigation condition with requirement to supply ratio above 1 (Figures 1.7 to 1.10).

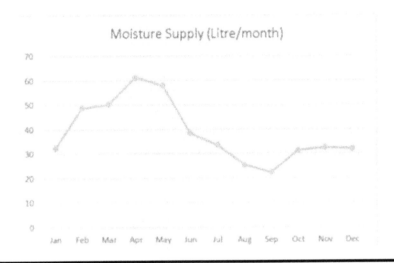

Figure 1.7   Watering pattern followed for Subject C annually based on Ambe bahar.

Figure 1.8   Requirement to supply ratio for Subject C.

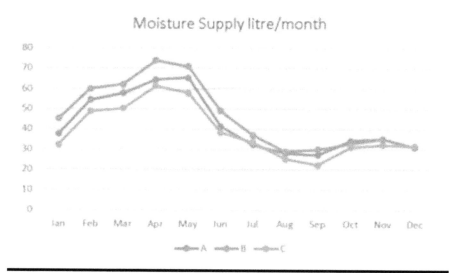

Figure 1.9 **Comparison of all three subjects based on annual watering pattern.**

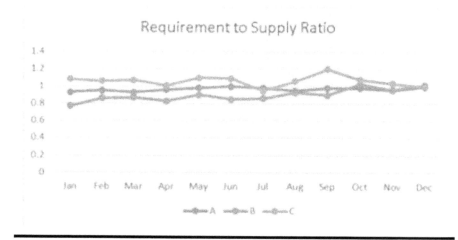

Figure 1.10 **Comparison of all three subjects based on requirement to supply ratio.**

1.6.2 Part B for Implementation of Prediction Model

Once the datasets are trained to consider the irrigation patterns for the ideal fruit condition, the prediction model begins to predict the requirements (Table 1.5). The following table shows the prediction of requirements and supply initiated. The following model is trained for the Ambe bahar flowering pattern (Figures 1.11 to 1.13).

Table 1.5 Prediction Model Result Table

Time	Prediction of Requirement (L/month)	Moisture Supply
January	35	35
February	52	52
March	54	54
April	62	62
May	64	64
June	42	42
July	32	32
August	27	27
September	27	27
October	34	34
November	34	34
December	32	32

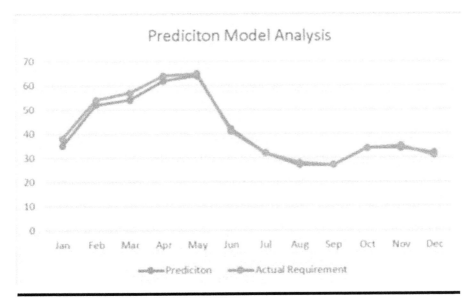

Figure 1.11 Water supply based on prediction model.

Figure 1.12   Requirement to supply ratio based on prediction model.

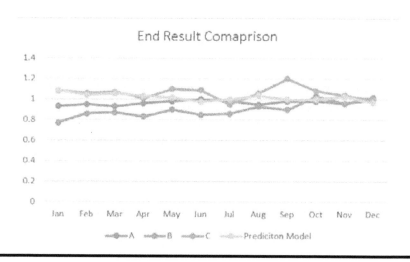

Figure 1.13   End result comparison of requirement to supply ratio with the requirement to supply ratio of ideal, cracked, and water-deprived fruit.

Due to following the discussed prediction model, the tree produced a yield of 8.4 kg. There were 10% fruit with a weight of 200 gm, 67% of fruit with a weight of around 250 gm, 9% fruit with weight of 275 gm, and rest showed signs of cracking. This shows that the prediction model gave a yield with efficiency of 86–93% (including the some minor cracked fruits). The rainfall to that point in the site of investigation was around 561 mm. In the future scope of development, the prediction model can become more accurate with integration of the climatic factors from the Indian Meteorological Department. One concern which still lingers in the prediction model is the consideration of water backflow in rainy conditions. Another important aspect is the irregularities being posed in the monsoon pattern. Since the investigation site was away from any natural water reserve, no problem was encountered due to groundwater rise or fall. Over a period of time, datasets will be trained for the other two flowering seasons as well.

1.7 Conclusion

The results clearly show that the prediction model was able to give us an 85% yield of 85% commercial grade. In order to achieve this result, the Naïve Bayes algorithm successfully predicted the requirement of water for the plants and provided precise supply. This model avoided the wastage of water that may happen during the irrigation. Though drip irrigation is considered to be highly efficient in saving water, the precision model helps us to understand the change in water requirements based on the flowering cycle. This adds to the benefits of drip irrigation and provides a much more efficient supply. Pomegranate is an all-year blooming fruit. The flowering seasons occur in different climatic seasons, thereby imposing differences in the requirements. However, these differences are eliminated using our proposed model which otherwise requires human intervention even in drip irrigation. Further, this work can be extended by adding an algorithm for prediction of diseases of plants.

1.8 Future Work

In the practice we have outlined, it is very well mentioned the use of the Naïve Bayes algorithm to predict the water requirement of the crop. However, the health of a crop is not dependent only on the water being fed to it or the watering pattern being followed. A crop requires thorough monitoring throughout its lifecycle. For pomegranates, the flowering and fruiting period is the most important phase. This is also the time when the pomegranate plant is most vulnerable to disease attacks or requires nutrients to grow. Under such circumstances, if the requirements of the plant are monitored using appropriate sensors, then our algorithm can be modified and used to fulfill these requirements. These requirements include the spraying of pesticides and insecticides in the advent of pest or insect attacks. Simultaneously the fertilizers can also be provided to the soil based on the nutrient value data. Thereby appropriate care can be taken of the plant. The collection of all these datasets and accordingly training the datasets will help the farmers also to predict the final health and yield of the orchards. This will help them to further plan their financial activities more precisely.

References

1. https://icar.org.in/files/Vision-2050-ICAR.pdf
2. http://apeda.in/agriexchange/Market%20Profile/one/POMEGRANATE.aspx
3. www.indiatoday.in/india/story/tamil-nadu-andhra-pradesh-water-dispute-palar-river-1573564-2019-07-25
4. www.thehindu.com/news/cities/Visakhapatnam/water-scarcity-stares-at-coastal-andhra/article22819788.ece
5. www.globalcitizen.org/en/content/india-farmers-water-loss-food-security/#:~:text=Of%20the%20245%20billion%20cubic,because%20of%20lack%20of%20ra infall
6. https://indianexpress.com/article/cities/pune/as-production-hit-by-moisture-stress-pomegranate-farmers-in-maharashtra-share-woes-of-mango-growers-5792087/
7. Malche, T., & Maheshwary, P. (2017). Internet of Things (IoT) based water level monitoring system for smart village. In: Modi, N., Verma, P., & Trivedi, B. (eds) Proceedings of International Conference on Communication and Networks. Advances in Intelligent Systems and Computing, vol 508. Springer, Singapore. https://doi.org/10.1007/978-981-10-2750-5_32
8. Tsouros, D., Bibi, S., & Sarigiannidis, P. (2019). A review on UAV-based applications for precision agriculture. Information, vol. 10, no. 11, p. 349. https://doi.org/10.3390/info10110349
9. Choi, C., Kim, J., Han, H., Han, D., & Kim, H. (2019). Development of water level prediction models using machine learning in wetlands: A case study of upo wetland in South Korea. Water, vol. 12, no. 1, p. 93. https://doi.org/10.3390/w12010093
10. http://fruitandnuteducation.ucdavis.edu/fruitnutproduction/Pomegranate/Pomegranate_Pests_Deficiencies/Pomegranate_Diseases_Disorders/
11. Nageswara Rao, R., & Sridhar, B. (2018). IoT based smart crop-field monitoring and automation irrigation system. In 2018 2nd International Conference on Inventive Systems and Control (ICISC) (pp. 478–483). IEEE. https://doi.org/10.1109/ICISC.2018.8399118
12. Gutiérrez, J., Villa-Medina, J. F., Nieto-Garibay, A., & Porta-Gándara, M. Á. (2014). Automated irrigation system using a wireless sensor network and GPRS module. IEEE Transactions on Instrumentation and Measurement, vol. 63, no. 1, pp. 166–176. https://doi.org/10.1109/TIM.2013.2276487
13. Ahmed, N., De, D., & Hussain, I. (2018). Internet of Things (IoT) for smart precision agriculture and farming in rural areas. IEEE Internet of Things Journal, vol. 5, no. 6, pp. 4890–4899. https://doi.org/10.1109/JIOT.2018.2879579
14. Patil, G., Gawande, P., & Bag, R. (2017). Smart agriculture system based on IoT and its social impact. International Journal of Computer Applications, vol. 176 no. 1, 0975–8887.
15. Jacquline, M., Suseno, N., & Manaha, R. (2019). Automatic watering system for plants with IoT monitoring and notification. CogITo Smart Journal, vol. 4, p. 316. https://doi.org/10.31154/cogito.v4i2.138.316–326
16. Shah, K., Pawar, S., Prajapati, G., & Upadhyay, S., & Hegde, G. (2019, March 26). Proposed automated plant watering system using IoT. Proceedings 2019: Conference on Technologies for Future Cities (CTFC). https://ssrn.com/abstract=3360353; http://dx.doi.org/10.2139/ssrn.3360353
17. Adiat, K. A. N., Ajayi, O. F., Akinlalu, A. A., & Tijani, I. B. (2020). Prediction of groundwater level in basement complex terrain using artificial neural network: A case of Ijebu-Jesa, southwestern Nigeria. Applied Water Science, vol. 10, p. 8. https://doi.org/10.1007/s13201-019-1094-6

18. Meshram, D., Gorantiwar, S., Mittal, H. K., Singh, N., & Lohkare, A. S. (2013). Water requirement of pomegranate (Punica granatum L.) plants upto five year age. Journal of Applied Horticulture, vol. 14, pp. 47–50. https://doi.org/10.37855/jah.2012.v14i01.08

19. Singh, A., Burman, U., Santra, P., & Morwal, B. R. (2017). Fruit cracking of pomegranate and its relationship with temperature and plant water status in hot arid region of India. Journal of Agrometeororology, vol. 16, pp. 24–29.

Chapter 2

A Brief Review on Lightweight Practice of Docker Vulnerabilities

Ayush Pritam Bage, Sameer Saxena, and Yudhveer Singh

2.1 Introduction

Docker is an open source platform for running applications and making the development and distribution process easier. The apps created with Docker are bundled with all necessary dependencies into a common format known as a container. These containers continue to execute in isolation on top of the kernel of the operating system. The additional layer of abstraction may have an influence on performance.

Even though container technologies have existed for over a decade, Docker, a relatively new programme, is now a standout amongst the top inventions, since it incorporates additional capacities that previous technologies did not have. Initially, it allows you to construct and govern containers.

These virtualized programmes may be used everywhere without any modifications. Furthermore, on the identical hardware, Docker can express more virtual scenarios than alternative innovations. To summarize, Docker may easily collaborate with third-party instruments that aid in the deployment and management of Docker containers. Docker containers are simple to deploy in a cloud-based system.

DOI: 10.1201/9781003441601-2

2.2 Docker Weakness

Because they enable users to execute numerous apps on the same host operating system, Docker containers are already in high demand. It manages a variety of operating system isolation and security measures as well; however, a problem occurs when these Docker images are unsafe, which results in dangers and other significant security problems. To get around or make these container images more stable, they should be studied statically. The aforementioned container approach should be implemented prior to the container's execution so that potential threats may be neutralized without harming the software.

Docker technology is relatively simple in terms of security for container images. We also typically do not need to be concerned about APIs for instance network overlays or because the analysis is performed after the container image is produced, i.e., prior to container execution, "composite software-defined storage configurations" are not a substantial component of the analyzing phase.

In the first incidence, "Docker" was formed in March 2012, with the revelation of a new method termed containerization, which led to "virtualization at the OS level". Docker contributes to a lightweight and fast environment [1]. Docker is frequently portrayed as a simple virtual machine (VM), although this is not the case. It is not the same as a VM.

Docker allows you to interact with infrastructure in the same manner that you would work with apps, by including image building instructions in a "Dockerfile" and maintaining image version control.

Furthermore, it has the option to raise or reduce resources as well as scalability to run on many platforms. Containers are not a novel concept, but Docker technology simplifies their implementation [3]. Furthermore, it is vital to recognize that while working with pictures, these images may include vulnerabilities.

The container's primary priority is security. There are serious security concerns concerning containers, such as the security concerns that occur when a user uploads self-made machine that other users don't know is really safe to install or not. It is critical to understand that content of container images must be carefully specified. Containerization security management differs from that of conventional standard apps (Table 2.1).

Table 2.1   Distinction between Container and Virtual Machine [2]

Docker Containers	*Virtual Machines*
Process isolation at the OS level	Process isolation on hardware
Are widely available if already constructed	Are difficult to find ready-made
Boots in seconds	Boots in minutes
Uses less resources	Uses more resources

There are two sort of security checks that may be performed: dynamic security analysis and static security analysis. If both the methods are used it is possible to determine if any of the container images include problems. According to a poll conducted in January 2014, the companies stated that security was a major issue. This is due to the fact that containers rely on the base image, and images may include "vulnerabilities" that can spread to every container.

Docker outperforms previous virtual approaches in terms of performance. When analyzing Docker image security, there are a few things to consider. From the security perspective, the best option for a base image is an empty container or "distroless" (a collection of images generated by Google), or UBI given by reputable vendors like Red Hat and IBM that were designed with security in mind.

2.3 Methodology

Various picture security analysis approaches have been utilized in recent years with the goal of achieving optimum solutions to these security concerns. This section assesses various analytical methodologies. The methodology used in this research is the product of our effort in conjunction with the results of earlier analytical methodologies. Socchi performed the most current Docker image analysis. They offer knowledge regarding security measures developed by Docker Inc., as well as information about verified and certified images that might increase Docker Hub security. Furthermore, they identified the distribution of all vulnerabilities among repository types (Table 2.2).

Table 2.2   Listing of Tools to Check the Vulnerabilities in Images [3]

Tools	Working
Docker Bench for Security	A tool for comparing Docker containers to security specifications; its tests are based on the industry-standard CIS benchmark
Cilium	Focuses on network connection security
Anchore	A container security inspection tool that employs CVE data as well as user-defined rules
Clair	CoreOS-developed static analysis of container vulnerability
Notary	A container security framework that incorporates a server with cryptographic responsibilities
BanyanOps Collector	A static analysis framework for Docker container images or registries
Grafes	An API for assisting with and analyzing internal security policies

The container will be able to customize the sensitive data of additional containers that target the application's integrity and other data. Furthermore, these containers may include comparable assaults to another "semi-honest" container, which will lead to targeting of another container. Our objective is to guard against attacks that will target other containers and cause problems in various ways. To secure the containers from various dangers and assaults, "statically analyze" the images so that no threats may be found after the execution process.

One prevalent misunderstanding is that "containers genuinely contain". However, containers are merely another kind of virtualization and do not truly protect the system from rogue applications since not all of the resources to which the container has access are namespace. Docker security is all about decreasing the likelihood of such attacks as described, as well as reducing the host kernel's attack surface. A plethora of container vulnerabilities are being addressed and resolved as Docker improves.

2.4 Contaminated Images

The official website for Docker Hub has over a million of images but as such there is no pledge that the image was obtained from a reliable root. An intruder may include malicious code with the picture to get access to the machine and the data contained inside. There is also the chance that the photos are out of current, and that many of them have vulnerabilities. Many attempts have been made to fix this issue, and the most recent version of Docker includes a new security feature in which image IDs represent the content contained within the image [4].

Docker Cloud, a hosted service that provides a registry with building and testing tools for Dockerized application images, can scan images in private repositories to ensure that they are free of known security vulnerabilities or exposures and publish the scan findings for each image tag [5]. This security scanner, on the other hand, was free for subscribers to private repositories until August 1, 2016.

2.5 Vulnerability of Images

The emphasis is on the factors that make photos more susceptible, as well as how these difficulties are addressed by other analytic tools. The following are the root reasons of Docker image and repository vulnerability:

- Insecure image creation
- Untrusted image cryptographic configuration creation
- Fault in picture distribution, verification, storage, and decompression are all possible
- Back doors inside images
- Threats might be related to Docker or libcontainer

It is critical not to put your confidence in any photos or archives obtained on the Internet. Docker currently funds a crew solely dedicated to reviewing and publishing images in official repositories [6]. Twenty-three per cent of total images from the Docker core are labelled as the most recent; these images also include a significant number of vulnerabilities.

2.6 Docker Architecture

Docker operates on a "client-server architecture". The Docker client communicates with the Docker daemon, which builds, executes, and distributes your Docker containers [7]. A Docker client can connect to a distant Docker daemon, or the client and daemon are utilizing the same operating system. Docker's design allows it to share resources with the OS kernel and access data within containers.

2.7 Threats to Validity

Internal Validity: Because this study relies heavily on hand labelling, the results may be subjective. To avoid this risk, I performed multiple rounds tagging in side by side, accompanied by talks to increase the findings' acceptance. For example, we conducted half of the labelling concurrently, then reviewed and discussed the findings. We continued up to 75% once we agreed on the results, followed by debates and evaluations, until we ultimately obtained 100% labelling (Figure 2.1).

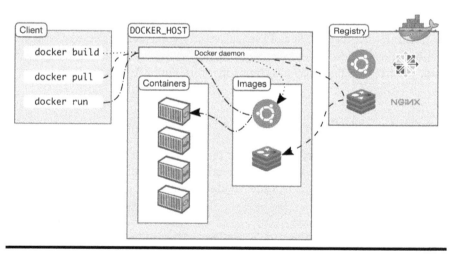

Figure 2.1   Docker architecture.

Source: Adapted from www.researchgate.net/figure/High-level-overview-of-Docker-architecture_fig1_308050257

Exterior Validity: Our chosen projects are relevant to many areas of machine learning. However, our findings may not be applicable to all ML-based software initiatives. We made our dataset available online. Future research is encouraged to replicate and confirm our findings in various types of ML-based software initiatives [8].

2.8 HelloBench

HelloBench is a new norm developed to test container launch. HelloBench natively performs Docker operations, allowing you to measure pushes, pulls, and runs individually. The benchmark consists of two parts: a collection of container images and a test harness for performing fundamental operations in such containers.

As of June 1, 2015, the most recent were the images from the Docker Hub collection. HelloBench is made up of 57 of the 72 photos that were accessible at the time. We chose images that could be run with minimal configuration and did not rely on other containers. WordPress, for instance, is not included since a WordPress container is dependent on a separate MySQL container [9].

2.9 Containerization

Some challenges arise as a result of virtualization, such as resource constraints, insecurity, and isolation. We can think of containerization as the next virtualization; if we want to run an application, we don't need to install the necessary operating system and dependencies; instead, we just need to package the programme with the operating system libraries and dependencies—these are required to run the application in any environment—in one container, which can be shipped and downloaded anywhere and at any time [10].

Dayo, Alowolodu Olufunso in 2021 propose a multi-containerized application utilizing Docker containers and Kubernetes clusters; this paper discussed the creation and deployment of applications in manufacturing and development settings, which provided a significant challenge [11]. The deployed software is provided at a slower rate and at a greater maintenance expense. Docker and Kubernetes will be used to mitigate this, and the Fibonacci sequence calculator will be used to test it. All the program instances in any application are done using Docker Compose [12].

2.10 Conclusion

Various technologies are being used to do a comparative examination for the security of Docker images. The security measures are also mentioned, which are implemented using various tools and software developed by various platforms to make containers that are safer and more dependable. Furthermore, establishing secure container images should be done with caution so that threats do not become a big worry for containers [13]. Docker containers were beset by security vulnerabilities in their early days. Docker containers have not been utilized in the production environment due to security concerns. One of the most serious difficulties was the lack of user namespaces [10].

References

[1] https://docs.docker.com/get-started/overview/

[2] Jain, Vipin, et al. "Static vulnerability analysis of docker images." IOP Conference Series: Materials Science and Engineering 1131.1 (2021).

[3] www.ibm.com/cloud/learn/docker

[4] Upadhya, Sahana, et al. "A state-of-art review of docker container security issues and solutions." American International Journal of Research in Science, Technology, Engineering and Mathematics 17 (2017): 33–36.

[5] https://techbeacon.com/security/17-open-source-container-security-tools

[6] Openja, M., et al. "Studying the practices of deploying machine learning projects on docker." Proceedings of the 26th International Conference on Evaluation and Assessment in Software Engineering (pp. 190–200), 2022, June.

[7] Mouat, Adrian. Docker Security: Using Containers Safely in Production. O'Reilly Media, 2015.

[8] Huang, Delu, et al. "Security analysis and threats detection techniques on docker container." 2019 IEEE 5th International Conference on Computer and Communications (ICCC). IEEE, 2019.

[9] Wist, Katrin, and Malene Helsem. "Vulnerability landscape in docker hub images." Master's thesis, Norwegian University of Science and Technology (NTNU), 2020.

[10] Merkel, D. "Docker: lightweight linux containers for consistent development and deployment." Linux Journal, 239 (2014): 2.

[11] Rad, Babak Bashari, et al. "An introduction to docker and analysis of its performance." International Journal of Computer Science and Network Security (IJCSNS) 17.3 (2017): 228.

[12] Bolton, B. "Ladder and functional block programing." Journal of Sports Science and Medicine (2006): 453–481.

[13] Zhang, Yao, and S. Wang. "Research on docker security." Network Security Technology & Application (2017): 32–33.

Chapter 3

Deep Learning-Based Serverless Image Handler Using Amazon Web Services

Parul Dubey, Pushkar Dubey, and
Kailash Kumar Sahu

3.1 Introduction

Signal processing is a discipline of mathematics and electrical engineering that investigates the analysis and processing of analogue and digital signals. It also explores how signals are stored and processed in various ways, such as filtering and other operations on signals. These signals include, but are not limited to, transmission signals, sound or voice signals, picture signals, and other signals, amongst other types of information.

Image processing is the area of signal processing that is concerned with signals whose input is an image and whose output is also an image, among all of these signals. As its name suggests, it is concerned with image processing. For the uninitiated, image processing is the act of taking a picture and transforming it into a digital format that allows specific tasks to be done on the image. A video frame or an image are examples of inputs that may be used to create outputs that are in the form of video frames or picture characteristics, respectively. The vast majority of the time, an image processing system interprets pictures as two equal symbols to which it applies a set of algorithms.

DOI: 10.1201/9781003441601-3

It is one of the most rapidly increasing technologies accessible today, owing to its vast use across a wide range of industry sectors. Graphic design is a primary focus of engineering and computer science research centres around the country [1, 2]. These are the three primary steps of image processing: acquisition, processing, and display. Importing a picture may be accomplished by digital photography and/or an optical scanner. Images are analyzed and managed in a variety of ways, including via the use of visual detection patterns such as those observed in satellite photography. In the last step, it produces a picture or a report that may be utilized for additional research and investigation. Image processing may be used to improve the quality of photos or to collect warnings from images that can then be fed into algorithms that predict the future. Further, it may be separated into two categories: analogue image processing and digital image processing.

The phrase "analogue image processing" refers to the alteration of pictures by electrical means. The most common example of this is a television show, which is shown almost every day. The amplitude of voltage levels varies to represent visible brightness in a television stream, and the voltage levels themselves fluctuate [3]. The look of the shown picture may be altered by electronically altering the signal being displayed. It is possible to brighten, darken, or modify the brightness range of the projected image by adjusting the amplitude and reference signals of the video signal, which is controlled by the TV's brightness and contrast settings. Analog signals are employed in the processing of analogue images. Analog signals are processed in two dimensions when they are received. Images are altered electrically in this kind of processing, which is accomplished by modifying the electrical signal.

Digital image processing has progressively displaced analogue image processing in the business as a result of the greater variety of applications available.

3.1.1 Digital Image Processing

Images are characterized as two-dimensional functions, $F(x,y)$, in which the amplitude of F at any pair of spatial coordinates (x,y) is referred to as intensity. Images are represented as two- dimensional functions, $F(x,y)$. A digital picture is one that has finite x, y, and amplitude values, as opposed to a traditional image. An image may be defined as a two-dimensional array with rows and columns.

There are many different types of images, listed here:

1. Binary images have only two pixel components, 0 and 1. This is why they are referred to as binary images in their name. This photograph is also known as a monochrome photograph.
2. "Black-and-white picture" is the name given to an image that is entirely black and white.
3. The 8-bit colour format is the most extensively used photo format on the market today. It is referred to as a "grayscale image" due to the fact that it

comprises 256 different shades of grey. Among the numbers 0 and 255 are the representations of black and white, respectively, while the value 127 is the representation of grey.

4. Colour photos are stored in the colour format (16-bit), which is a 16-bit colour depth. It features a total of 65,536 different colour variations. This format is also known as "high colour format" in certain circles. When comparing a colour image in this format to a grayscale image, there is a notable change in the distribution of the colours. There are three different 16-bit formats: red, green, and blue. This well-known RGB encoding scheme is used in many applications.

Individual pieces of a digitized picture, each having its own unique value and location in the image, come together to form the image [4, 5]. This group of components is referred to as picture elements, image elements, and pixels, among other things. The pixels of a digital picture are most often used to distinguish between the image's component pieces. The field of digital image processing is primarily concerned with the development of a digital system that can perform operations on a digital image.

In this scenario, image processing is carried out on digital computers to save time. In order to convert the original image to digital form, a scanner–digitizer will be used, after which the image will be processed. The definition refers to a sequence of operations on numerical representations of things, which is what is intended by the term. Beginning with a single image and ending with a different image is the goal of this technique. After then, using this process, one picture may be converted into another. Digital image processing is the process of manipulating a two-dimensional picture with the use of a digital computer, as opposed to a traditional computer. Any two-dimensional data can be processed digitally in a broader sense than it is currently possible. Arrays of real numbers are represented by a small number of bits in a digital image, which is why they are so useful. Digital image processing technologies are the most effective when it comes to adaptability, reproducibility, and the preservation of the accuracy of the original dataset.

3.2 Related Work

Noise is present at all stages of the digital photography process, including capture, coding, transmission, and processing. Digital images including noise are very difficult to clean up unless the photographer is acquainted with the noise modelling process. As a result, while researching image denoising algorithms, it is critical to consider the effects of noise models. One such paper provides an overview of numerous noise models, each of which is made explicit [6]. It is possible to establish the source of these noise models. The next part contains a thorough and quantitative evaluation of the noise models that are available in digital pictures.

A fundamental introduction to medical image processing via the use of deep learning is the purpose of some research [7]. The popularity of deep learning may be attributed to a variety of computer science breakthroughs, among which are a number of other factors. Moving on to the principles of perceptron and neural networks, They made a better understanding of why deep learning has grown so popular across a broad variety of application domains as a result of this analysis. Medical image processing, in particular picture recognition and identification, segmentation, image registration, and computer-aided diagnosis, has undoubtedly been significantly influenced by this rapid growth. Surprising results have been obtained in the physical sciences via the use of simulated, training, and reconstruction approaches.

It is difficult to apply trained GAN models to practical image processing, despite the success of generative adversarial networks (GANs) in picture synthesis. Back-propagation or the learning of an additional encoder were often used in previous systems to flip a target image back to the latent space. But the reconstructions produced by each of the techniques fall well short of being optimum. mGANprior is a novel approach developed by researchers that allows us to integrate well-trained GANs as effective prior to a wide variety of image processing jobs [8]. To be more explicit, they used numerous latent codes to construct different feature maps at an intermediate layer of the generator, which they subsequently combine with adaptive channel significance to recover the input image. The quality of the image reconstruction is significantly improved as a result of the over-parameterization of the latent space, which outperforms existing competitors. After training GAN models, they may be used to perform a variety of real-world tasks such as image colourization, super resolution, image inpainting, semantic alteration, and other tasks that require high-fidelity picture reconstruction. They do so to investigate the characteristics of the layer-wise representation learned by GAN models, as well as the information that may be conveyed by each layer of the representation.

One of the papers provides an overview of the new technologies and theoretical concepts that have emerged to explain the rise of computer vision, particularly as it relates to image processing, and how they are being used in a variety of fields [9]. Researchers used computer vision to review images and videos in order to acquire essential information, interpret information from events or descriptions, and identify patterns in the landscape. It made use of a multi-range application domain strategy in conjunction with extensive data analysis. This research offered a contribution of current advancements on reviews related to computer vision, image processing, and their related issues, as well as a summary of previous advancements. Researchers divided the computer vision mainstream into four categories, such as image processing, object identification, and machine learning, for convenience. They also provided a succinct summary of the most recent information available on the techniques and their performance.

Using the COVID-19 dataset, in a paper researchers started by summarizing the present state of deep learning applications for medical image processing, which will serve as the foundation for the remainder of their work. Following that, there is a discussion of deep learning and its use in healthcare during the previous decade or so. Next, three examples of deep learning applications for COVID-19 medical image processing are shown, with the first two coming from China and the third from Korea. Numerous obstacles and issues with deep learning implementations for COVID-19 medical image processing have been identified, and it is projected that more study is conducted in the management of the outbreak and crisis, which will result in the development of smart healthy cities.

The Internet of Things (IoT) has touched a broad variety of businesses since its introduction. The cloud gets hyperspectral images (HSIs) from the Earth observation system's hyperspectral sensors. Edge servers assess data using AI models, resulting in speedier response times and cheaper costs. A basic AI concept known as subspace clustering may be used to evaluate hyperspectral photographs and other high-dimensional picture data. Due to the fact that they are constructed on a single model, existing subspace clustering approaches are prone to noise. The connectivity and sparsity of the representation coefficient matrix are not well- balanced. One such work offered a subspace clustering algorithm with a post-processing approach that takes into consideration connectivity and sparsity [10]. The selection of close neighbours, defined as those with a high coefficient and common neighbours, is carried out using a non-dominated sorting algorithm. The coefficients between the near and sample neighbours are used to prune away any connections that are redundant, erroneous, or reserved for the model's internal use, if any. Finally, the post-processing approach allows for inter- and intra-subspace couplings. The recommended postprocessing algorithms for IoT and picture identification are compared to the current methodologies to verify their effectiveness and generality. The experimental results have shown that the recommended approach may boost the accuracy of noisy data clustering in the IoT setting.

Photoacoustic imaging (PAI) is a kind of imaging technology that is dependent on the PA effect. As a consequence of the absorption of electromagnetic radiation by exogenous contrast agents and/or endogenous substances present in the biological tissue, ultrasonic waves are generated. Because of PAI's high acoustic spatiotemporal resolution and good optical contrast, it is feasible to view absorbers deep inside structures without inflicting any damage. It follows that, as a consequence of optical diffusion and ultrasonic attenuation in turbid biological tissue, the quality of PA images degrades with time. In order to generate high-quality images that show structural and functional features in the deep tissues, PAI depends on sophisticated signal and image processing technologies, which are described in detail in a research paper [11]. They illustrated how photoacoustic imaging is strongly reliant on the usage of image processing, which is a key component of the technique.

Particle geometry techniques, including one that calculates the form factor, are detailed in one of the paper and may be used to simulate a wide range of physical separation processes. The performance of the image processing approach was evaluated by the use of a sieving experiment on a sample of abandoned electric equipment [12]. When comparing the results of the image processing and sieving experiments, it was discovered that the size error width between them increased the value of aspect ratio and circularity when compared to each other. Particle shape was used to establish the most suitable treatment technique, and an overall conceptual flowsheet was developed to accomplish this.

Deep learning and image processing algorithms are being used by researchers, experts, and businesses all over the world to analyze hundreds of X-ray and computed tomography (CT) images in real time. These algorithms are being implemented by researchers, experts, and businesses all over the world to accelerate the detection of pneumonia, including SARS, COVID-19, and other emerging strains. Medical image analysis, one of the most promising topics of research, is currently being used to identify and treat illnesses like MERS, COVID-19, and other contagious diseases. By comparing the performance of recent deep convolutional neural network architectures for automatically binary classifying pneumonia images, researchers used fine-tuned versions of the VGG16, VGG19, DenseNet201, Inception ResNet V2, Inception ResNet V3, Resnet50, MobileNet V2, and Xception networks, along with retraining a baseline CNN, to compare the performance of recent deep convolutional neural network architectures for instantaneously binary classifying pneumonia pictures. A total of 6,087 images from chest X-rays and CT scans were utilized to evaluate the proposed research.

In order to ensure global food security and long-term agricultural sustainability, it is necessary to recognize water stress as early as possible. While there are several ways for detecting agricultural water stress, many of them are time-consuming and difficult to apply, owing to the high degree of complexity necessary in the sensors or equipment used to detect the condition. With the help of image processing, it is possible to assess water stress in real time [13]. Machine learning, combined with traditional image processing, improves the capacity of traditional image processing to detect water stress. Image classification has been more popular in recent years, thanks to the usage of convolutional neural networks (CNNs) based on deep learning (DL) [13]. One of the research studies looked at three crops: maize (*Zea mays*), okra (*Abelmoschus esculentus*), and soybean to determine whether three different deep learning models, AlexNet, GooLeNet, and Inception V3, could identify water stress in the field. For each crop, a total of 1,200 digital photographs were taken, which were then used to train the deep learning models. GoogLeNet's accuracy ratings for maize, okra, and soybean were 98.3%, 97.5%, and 94.1%, respectively, greater than those of the other two models in each of these categories.

3.3 Image Processing Procedures

Step-by-step instructions on how to do this are provided here.

- **Image Acquisition:** Digital picture processing starts here. Detection of particular photographs, such as a true or actual scenario inside arrangement of an object, using digital image detection. Processing, crowded storage, printing, and presenting these photographs are commonly accepted by this terminology [14, 15]. Acquiring photos could be disheartening when one considers the digital form in which they already exist.

- **Image Enhancement:** Digital images may be made better by modifying them to make them more suitable for display or analysis, among other things. Because we can turn off the music, sharpen the image, or turn on the picture, it is easier to distinguish important features.

- **Image Restoration:** A corrupt/noisy image is taken and measured against a new, unused image in the process of picture restoration. Motion blurring, sound, and camera focus are examples of ways in which exploitation might take place. The purpose of image restoration techniques is to reduce noise while recovering the resolution that has been lost.

- **Colouring Image Processing:** When working with colour images, a full understanding of light physics as well as colour vision physiology is essential. Material, building materials, food, places, and times of day are all distinguished by the colour of the material or construction material. Colour is used in the image processing process to distinguish between different pictures.

- **Wavelets Processing and Multiple Solutions:** While decorating a shot with clouds, trees, and flowers, one will use a different level brush depending on the size of the topographies. Brushes and wavelets are similar in that they are connected to one other. The method of transforming photos using wavelets is a helpful tool. It is feasible to study several image solutions by using the wavelet transform.

- **Image Compression:** Digital photography is primarily reliant on picture compression, which lowers the total cost of storing and transmitting photographs while increasing their quality. Due to the complex consequences of traditional pressure techniques, visual awareness and asset data image assets may be gained as a result of the resulting benefits.

- **Character Recognition:** In the case of scanned images or written text, computer- readable text is the outcome of optical character binding, often known as OCR, which is a machine-operated or electronic replacement of the images or text. The existence of information is often provided through data sources such as paper invoices, bank account statements, income, business cards, the number of printed records, or email, which may be accessed as soon as a new data source becomes accessible. They are often produced in this manner, and include digitally printed manuscripts that may be sorted, searched, and stored electronically by machine processes such as machine conversion and display online, text to voice, retrieval of key data, and text mining. OCR does research on intelligence, patterns, and computing ideas, among other things.

3.4 Role of Machine Learning and Deep Learning in Image Processing

3.4.1 Machine Learning

In the realm of automation, machine learning (ML) has evolved as a prominent AI technique applied by a wide spectrum of enterprises and individuals. As processing power and data accessibility both increase, practitioners are now able to create useful outputs in a range of domains. Image data may now be analyzed by ML systems in the same way as human brains do.

These may be found in nearly every part of our life, from our smart phones to our computers to our self-driving automobiles and beyond. There are four general types of machine learning, namely supervised learning, unsupervised learning, semi-supervised learning, and reinforced learning [16–19]. Figure 3.1 illustrates the many ML subcategories. This diagram displays the system's inputs, its learning process, and its outputs in three layers: top, middle, bottom.

3.4.1.1 Supervised Learning

A dataset comprising certain facts and associated tags is needed for this family of models. For example, photographs of animals may be used as observations, with the labels providing the animal's name [20, 21].

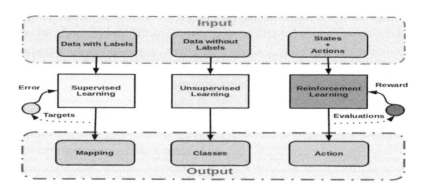

Figure 3.1   Categories of machine learning.

These models must first be trained on labelled datasets before they can predict future events. As a consequence of this strategy, the learning algorithm develops an inferred function that is then applied to fresh, unlabeled data that are placed into the model in order to govern the outcome of the recent results. After a significant amount of training, the algorithm is capable of setting goals for any incoming input. By comparing its output to the intended result (the ground truth label), the learning algorithm may also find and correct flaws, altering its output as required to reach the desired outcome (e.g., via back-propagation). Supervised modelling methodologies come into two categories: regression modelling and classification modelling.

3.4.1.2 Unsupervised Learning

There must be at least some observations in the dataset in order to apply this family of models, but it is not essential to know the labels or classes of those observations prior to applying this family of models. When processing data, it is vital that the data be labelled before processing so that computers may infer a function from unlabelled data in order to explain a concealed structure. Unlabelled data's hidden structures may be described using a data exploration approach and inferences from datasets, and the system may utilize data exploration and inferences from datasets to define the hidden structures of unlabelled data. Clustering and association models are subclasses of unsupervised learning and also its good examples.

3.4.1.3 Semi-Supervised Machine Learning

In both the supervised and unsupervised learning groups, the semi-supervised machine learning is an essential concept to understand. Semi-supervised models are trained using both labelled and unlabelled input to get the best results. It is ineffective to use supervised or unsupervised learning when the quantity of labelled data available is insufficient to compensate for the amount of unlabelled data available. Material that has not been properly categorized is often utilized to infer information about the individuals who are the subject of the investigation. The term "semi-supervised learning" refers to an approach that is generally considered to be effective. In contrast to traditional supervised learning, semi-supervised learning takes use of labelled data rather than random data, which distinguishes it from traditional supervised learning. In the same way that supervised learning includes more information than unsupervised learning, tagged data contains more information. Semi-supervised learning, in contrast to projected datasets, makes use of smaller labelled datasets to train the model.

3.4.1.4 Reinforced Learning

These algorithms utilize estimated mistakes as incentives or punishments to reward or penalize their users. If the fault is bad enough, the punishment will be severe and the reward will be little. As long as the fault is little, the penalty will be modest and the reward will be substantial.

When learning from data, machine learning algorithms often go through a series of phases known as a pipeline. Take, for example, a generic example of image processing and utilize it to build a working approach for that application scenario. In order to learn and predict outcomes with high accuracy, machine learning algorithms need a huge amount of high-quality data to be used. In order to get the best results, the photographs must be processed, labelled, and generalized for machine learning image processing. That is where computer vision (CV) comes in. Computer vision (CV) is the study of how computers can read pictures and recognize patterns in them. Using CV, we may process, load, convert, and edit photographs in order to provide the best possible dataset for the machine learning algorithm to learn from.

Consider the following scenario: we're trying to figure out if a photo includes a genuine dog or a cat, and we're constructing an algorithm to accomplish it. Taking images of dogs and cats will be necessary, and then preprocessing them using CV will be necessary. These are some of the pre-processing steps:

1. The format of all the photos can be changed to the same one.
2. Images may be edited by removing the superfluous parts.
3. Algorithms can learn from them by transforming ideas into numbers (array of numbers).

In a picture, the number of pixels that a computer can see in a picture is determined by the resolution of the image that is being supplied into the computer. Depending on the photo resolution, the height, width, and depth will be shown. It is therefore necessary to categorize fresh feature vectors using a machine-learning approach that is trained on a huge library of feature vectors whose classifications have previously been determined. In order to do this, we'll need to choose a suitable approach, such as Bayesian nets, decision trees, genetic algorithms, nearest neighbours, or neural networks, among others.

When specific parameters are included in the training data, the algorithms are able to learn from the patterns in the training data. We can, however, constantly fine-tune the trained model based on the performance data we gather and the results we get. We may also produce fresh predictions based on previously unobserved data by applying the trained model to new data.

3.4.2 Deep Learning

Deep learning is the only kind of machine learning that focuses on schooling the computer to mimic human behaviour, and it is the only type of machine learning that does so. As the term implies, deep learning refers to the process by which a computer system learns to perform classification tasks based on detailed input in the form of images or text, or even speech [22–24]. Such an algorithm has the potential to achieve accuracy that is comparable to or better than that of the state of the art (SOTA), and in certain cases, it may even outperform humans in terms of overall performance. In order to train them, a large quantity of labelled data is collected, as well as neural network topologies with several layers, which are used in conjunction with the labelled data to get the desired result. Some of the most important characteristics of DL are listed here.

- Virtual assistants, facial recognition, self-driving cars, and other comparable technologies all use deep learning as a foundation.
- It's a method of deep learning that begins with the collection of training data and ends with the use of the training's outputs.
- To describe the learning technique, the term "deep learning" has been adopted since the neural networks quickly learn about new layers of data that have been introduced to the dataset over the course of a single minute. To improve the system as a whole, all training is done with the goal of making it more efficient.
- Increased popularity among data professionals, along with increased data volume, has resulted in an increase in the system's training effectiveness and learning depth.

A particular kind of framework that imitates the human brain in terms of learning from data and generating models is known as a neural network. Convolution neural networks, sometimes known as CNNs, are a kind of neural network architecture that has made significant strides in the analysis of image data in recent years. The convolutional neural network is composed of three basic layers [25], which are as follows:

1. Convolutional Layer
2. Pooling Layer
3. Fully Connected Layer

- Convolutional Layer: The convolutional layer of CNN is responsible for the majority of the effort involved in recognizing properties in a given image. Following that, we choose random square blocks from the input image and apply a dot product with a filter on them (random filter size). A high output from the convolution layer is achieved when both matrices (the patch and the filter) have high values in the same locations (which gives the bright side of the image). If they don't, it will be very low (the dark side of the image). The dot product output of our filter may be able to tell us if the pixel pattern in our filter's output picture corresponds to the pixel pattern suggested by the underlying image or not.
- Pooling Layer: In the case of feature detection using convolutional layers, we end up with many feature maps as a result. These feature maps are created as

a result of the convolutional operation that is done between the input image and the filter during the processing step. As a result, we'll need to do another operation to lower the image's resolution. As a consequence, the "pooling" approach is utilized to reduce the number of pixel values in the arrays, which makes the learning process for the network simpler. They use two distinct approaches to spatially scale the input data, each of which operates separately on each depth slice:

- Max Pooling: This function returns the highest value from the range of the image defined by the kernel.
- Average Pooling: This function computes an image's average value by averaging the array's values throughout the image's whole range.

■ Fully Connected Layer: A fully connected layer (FC) is one in which each input is interconnected to every neuron in the network, resulting in a flattened input signal. Because they link the hidden layers with the output layer, end-of-network connectors may aid in the improvement of class scores.

3.5 Serverless Image Handler in AWS

This solution offers a serverless architecture in order to get started with low-cost image processing on the Amazon Web Services Cloud (AWS) [26–32]. With AWS for dynamic photo editing and Sharp open-source image processing tools, the concept achieves the best of both worlds [33]. Visitors to your websites and mobile applications will be more engaged if they make use of the solution's dynamic image management capabilities [34]. The serverless architecture shown in the Figure 3.2 can be deployed in minutes using AWS Cloud Formation and the accompanying implementation guide, and it can be configured in minutes.

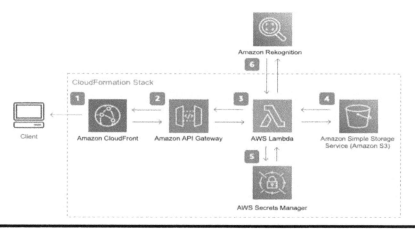

Figure 3.2 AWS Serverless Image Handler architecture.

Following the receipt of an HTTP request from a client device through CloudFront and API Gateway, the request is passed to the Lambda function for further processing. Rather than forwarding the request to the API Gateway, CloudFront will return the previously cached photo if a request for it was made before. This reduces the amount of time it takes to process the image and eliminates the cost associated with doing so as well.

If a request is received by API Gateway that has not yet been cached, the whole request is delivered to the Lambda function [35–37]. Sharp (open source image processing software) is used to modify the original picture stored in your Amazon S3 (Simple Storage Service) bucket into a modified version that can be utilized with the API Gateway [38, 39]. SIH also makes use of Thumbor to apply dynamic filters to the data. Additionally, as part of the solution, a CloudFront domain name with caching capabilities is established. CloudFront has now archived the updated image for easy retrieval and access in the future, should the need arise. By combining the solution's signed URL functionality with AWS Secrets Manager to encrypt the end-to-end request and response, users can prevent unauthorized use of their proprietary photographs.

SIH uses Amazon Rekognition to recognize faces in pictures submitted for smart cropping. This makes it easy to crop images to meet specific content or image criteria for certain content or images.

3.5.1 Rekognition

Because of Amazon Rekognition, one's apps may be able to benefit from powerful visual analysis. With Rekognition Image, anyone can quickly search, validate, and organize millions of images with ease. With the help of Rekognition Video, it is possible to extract motion-based context from archival or live-streamed videos. Rekognition Image is capable of recognizing objects, situations, and faces, as well as retrieving text and identifying celebrities, among other things. One may also use it to search individuals and compare their physical appearances with one another. In order to produce Rekognition Image, Amazon's computer vision experts used the same deep learning technology that they use to analyze billions of images every day for Prime Photos in order to create it.

Deep neural network models are used by Rekognition Image to detect and label hundreds of elements in your images, and AWS is continually adding additional labels and face recognition capabilities. With Rekognition Image, users only pay for the photographs they analyze and the face data they preserve, not for the software itself.

Rekognition Video, a video-recognition technology that recognizes people, objects, celebrities, and undesirable content in video feeds from Acuity, may be used to analyze Amazon S3 and live video feeds from Acuity. No matter whether their faces are not visible or if the whole person enters and departs the scene, Rekognition Video can still identify and track persons in films. If one has an app that notifies people instantly when an item is delivered to front door, this information may be incorporated in that app. Rekognition Video can index metadata such as objects, activities, sceneries, celebrities, and faces, which may then be searched for in video searches, allowing for faster results.

If deep learning systems are to provide trustworthy results on complex computer vision tasks such as object and scene identification, face analysis, and face recognition, they must be calibrated correctly, and they must be trained using large amounts of labelled ground truth data. Data sourcing, cleaning, and labelling is a time-consuming and expensive process that requires much effort. Aside from that, constructing a deep neural network is time-consuming and expensive since it necessitates the use of specialized hardware built around graphics processing units (GPU).

With Amazon Rekognition, customers won't have to waste time or money on constructing a deep learning pipeline since it will be completely managed and pre-trained for image and video recognition. Amazon Rekognition utilizes the most current research and gets new training data in order to maintain its models as accurate as possible. This saves more time so that one may devote it to the design and development of high-value apps.

As an S3 object, Amazon Rekognition Image can accept images with a maximum file size of 15 MB; as an image byte array, the maximum file size is 5 MB. Amazon Rekognition Image can accept pictures with a maximum file size of 5 MB [40]. Amazon Rekognition Video can handle up to 10 GB of data and six hours of video when stored as an S3 file. As a general rule of thumb, please make sure that the smallest object or face included in the photo is at least 5% of the size (in pixels) of the shortest image dimension. A minimum of 45 pixels broad or tall in each dimension is required for the smallest face or object when working with 1600x900 resolution photos.

3.6 Conclusion

Image processing is an important task at present. It makes use of deep leaning and machine learning algorithms. In this chapter we have studied the basics of images, image processing, machine learning, and deep learning. In the architecture discussed, we have simplified the burden of pipelining the deep learning algorithms by making use of AWS serverless platform. Rekognition is a service provided by AWS that makes use of deep learning and does image processing.

References

[1] Digital Image Processing Introduction. (n.d.). www.tutorialspoint.com/dip/image_processing_introduction.htm.

[2] Great Learning. (2021, June 11). Introduction to Image Processing | What Is Image Processing? *GreatLearning Blog: Free Resources What Matters to Shape Your Career!* www.mygreatlearning.com/blog/introduction-to-image-processing-what-is-image-processing/.

[3] Rao, K. M. M. Overview of Image Processing, Readings in Image Processing. https://www.drkmm.com/resources/ INTRODUCTION_TO_IMAGE_PROCESSING_29aug06.pdf.

[4] Wiley, V., & Lucas, T. (2018). Computer vision and image processing: A paper review. *International Journal of Artificial Intelligence Research*, 2(1), 29–36.

[5] Maier, A., Syben, C., Lasser, T., & Riess, C. (2019). A gentle introduction to deep learning in medical image processing. *Zeitschrift für Medizinische Physik*, 29(2), 86–101.

[6] Jiao, L., & Zhao, J. (2019). A survey on the new generation of deep learning in image processing. *IEEE Access*, 7, 172231–172263.

[7] Gu, J., Shen, Y., & Zhou, B. (2020). Image processing using multi-code gan prior. In *Proceedings of the IEEE/CVF conference on computer vision and pattern recognition* (pp. 3012–3021).

[8] Bhattacharya, S., Maddikunta, P. K. R., Pham, Q. V., Gadekallu, T. R., Chowdhary, C. L., Alazab, M., & Piran, M. J. (2021). Deep learning and medical image processing for coronavirus (COVID-19) pandemic: A survey. *Sustainable Cities and Society*, 65, 102589.

[9] https://arxiv.org/abs/1505.03489

[10] Bindhu, V., & Ranganathan, G. (2021). Hyperspectral image processing in internet of things model using clustering algorithm. *Journal of ISMAC*, 3(2), 163–175.

[11] Manwar, R., Zafar, M., & Xu, Q. (2021). Signal and image processing in biomedical photoacoustic imaging: A review. *Optics*, 2(1), 1–24.

[12] Kim, Y., & Dodbiba, G. (2021). A novel method for simultaneous evaluation of particle geometry by using image processing analysis. *Powder Technology*, 393, 60–73.

[13] El Asnaoui, K., Chawki, Y., & Idri, A. (2021). Automated methods for detection and classification pneumonia based on x-ray images using deep learning. In *Artificial intelligence and blockchain for future cybersecurity applications* (pp. 257–284). Cham: Springer.

[14] Chandel, N. S., Chakraborty, S. K., Rajwade, Y. A., Dubey, K., Tiwari, M. K., & Jat, D. (2021). Identifying crop water stress using deep learning models. *Neural Computing and Applications*, 33(10), 5353–5367.

[15] Sezer, A., & Altan, A. (2021). Detection of solder paste defects with an optimization-based deep learning model using image processing techniques. *Soldering & Surface Mount Technology*, 33(5), 291–298.

[16] Coca, G. L., Romanescu, Ş. C., Botez, Ş. M., & Iftene, A. (2020). Crack detection system in AWS cloud using convolutional neural networks. *Procedia Computer Science*, 176, 400–409.

[17] Mishra, N. K., & Celebi, M. E. (2016). An overview of melanoma detection in dermoscopy images using image processing and machine learning. arXiv:1601.07843.

[18] Mairal, J. (2010). Sparse coding for machine learning, image processing and computer vision (Doctoral dissertation, Cachan, Ecole Normale Supérieure).

[19] Machine Learning Image Processing. (2021, July 19). *AI & machine learning blog.* https://nanonets.com/blog/machine-learning-image-processing/.

[20] Hou, S., Feng, Y., & Wang, Z. (2017). Vegfru: A domain-specific dataset for fine-grained visual categorization. In *Proceedings of the IEEE international conference on computer vision* (pp. 541–549). New York: IEEE.

[21] Taher, K. A., Jisan, B. M. Y., & Rahman, M. M. (2019, January). Network intrusion detection using supervised machine learning technique with feature selection. In *2019 International conference on robotics, electrical and signal processing techniques (ICREST)* (pp. 643–646). New York: IEEE.

[22] Bhanu, K. N., Jasmine, H. J., & Mahadevaswamy, H. S. (2020, June). Machine learning Implementation in IoT based intelligent system for agriculture. In *2020 international conference for emerging technology (INCET)* (pp. 1–5). New York: IEEE.

[23] Ferreira, K. R., Queiroz, G. R., Camara, G., Souza, R. C. M., Vinhas, L., Marujo, R. F. B., . . . & Zaglia, M. C. (2020, March). Using remote sensing images and cloud services on AWS to improve land use and cover monitoring. In *2020 IEEE Latin American GRSS & ISPRS remote sensing conference (LAGIRS)* (pp. 558–562). New York: IEEE.

[24] Seal, A., & Mukherjee, A. (2019, April). Real time accident prediction and related congestion control using spark streaming in an AWS EMR cluster. In *2019 SoutheastCon* (pp. 1–7). New York: IEEE.

[25] Spillner, J., & Dorodko, S. (2017). Java code analysis and transformation into AWS lambda functions. arXiv:1702.05510.

[26] Pérez, A., Moltó, G., Caballer, M., & Calatrava, A. (2018). Serverless computing for container-based architectures. *Future Generation Computer Systems, 83*, 50–59.

[27] Amazon Rekognition—Frequently Asked Questions—AWS. (n.d.). *Amazon Web Services, Inc.* https://aws.amazon.com/rekognition/faqs/?nc=sn&loc=7.

[28] Monga, V., Li, Y., & Eldar, Y. C. (2021). Algorithm unrolling: Interpretable, efficient deep learning for signal and image processing. *IEEE Signal Processing Magazine, 38*(2), 18–44.

[29] Shao, Y., Di, L., Bai, Y., Guo, B., & Gong, J. (2012, August). Geoprocessing on the Amazon cloud computing platform—AWS. In *2012 first international conference on agro-geoinformatics (agro-geoinformatics)* (pp. 1–6). New York: IEEE.

[30] Guillermo, M., Billones, R. K., Bandala, A., Vicerra, R. R., Sybingco, E., Dadios, E. P., & Fillone, A. (2020, November). Implementation of automated annotation through mask RCNN object detection model in CVAT using AWS EC2 instance. In *2020 IEEE region 10 conference (TENCON)* (pp. 708–713). New York: IEEE.

[31] Baron, J., & Kotecha, S. (2013). *Storage options in the AWS cloud*. Washington, DC: Amazon Web Services.

[32] Chen, H., Wang, Y., Guo, T., Xu, C., Deng, Y., Liu, Z., . . . & Gao, W. (2021). Pre-trained image processing transformer. In *Proceedings of the IEEE/CVF conference on computer vision and pattern recognition* (pp. 12299–12310).

[33] Grzesik, P., & Mrozek, D. (2021, June). Serverless nanopore basecalling with AWS lambda. In *International conference on computational science* (pp. 578–586). Cham: Springer.

[34] Serverless Image Handler | Implementations | AWS Solutions. (n.d.). *Amazon Web Services, Inc.* https://aws.amazon.com/solutions/implementations/serverless-image-handler/#:~:text=The%20architecture%20combines%20AWS%20services,applications%20to%20drive%20user%20engagement.

[35] Risco, S., Moltó, G., Naranjo, D. M., & Blanquer, I. (2021). Serverless workflows for containerised applications in the cloud continuum. *Journal of Grid Computing, 19*(3), 1–18.

[36] Kumar, V. B., Kumar, S. S., & Saboo, V. (2016, September). Dermatological disease detection using image processing and machine learning. In *2016 third international conference on artificial intelligence and pattern recognition (AIPR)* (pp. 1–6). New York: IEEE.

[37] Jackson, K. R., Muriki, K., Ramakrishnan, L., Runge, K. J., & Thomas, R. C. (2011). Performance and cost analysis of the supernova factory on the amazon AWS cloud. *Scientific Programming, 19*(2–3), 107–119.

[38] Khan, A., Nawaz, U., Ulhaq, A., & Robinson, R. W. (2020). Real-time plant health assessment via implementing cloud-based scalable transfer learning on AWS DeepLens. *PLoS One, 15*(12), e0243243.

[39] Anteby, R., Horesh, N., Soffer, S., Zager, Y., Barash, Y., Amiel, I., . . . & Klang, E. (2021). Deep learning visual analysis in laparoscopic surgery: A systematic review and diagnostic test accuracy meta-analysis. *Surgical Endoscopy*, 1–13.

[40] Srinivasan, A., Natarajan, N., Karunakaran, R. V., Elangovan, R., Shankar, A., Sabharish, P. M., . . . & Radha, S. (2020, December). Elder care system using IoT and machine learning in AWS cloud. In *2020 IEEE 17th international conference on smart communities: Improving quality of life using ICT, IoT and AI (HONET)* (pp. 92–98). New York: IEEE.

Chapter 4

Ontology-Based Delegation Enforcement in the Cloud Ecosystem

Dimpy Jindal, Manju Kaushik, and Barkha Bahl

4.1 Introduction

In today's business world, there is a rising awareness of the significance of information as an essential resource for companies and other types of organizations. Better judgments, an improvement in competitiveness, and fewer mistakes are all goals that may be accomplished via the use of knowledge management, which aims to assist businesses in efficiently creating, deriving, sharing, and using information. A company requires intelligence on its rivals, partners, customers, and staff, in addition to intelligence about the circumstances of the market, future trends, and a great deal of other information, in order to operate its business operations more efficiently. On the current market, one can find a variety of solutions and technologies that provide assistance for more complex business process management. Companies anticipate that these apps will enable a diverse set of activities, including the development and analysis of company plans, the creation of customer-specific services, the execution of targeted marketing, and the forecasting of sales trends. In order to offer the proper degree of information support, many applications included inside the information system that support a broad variety of capabilities need to be interconnected. The use of ontologies and multi-agent systems is rapidly becoming one of the most popular strategies for the integration of information systems (MAS).

The MAS is made up of a collection of self-sufficient agents that are able to choose their own objectives and courses of action, as well as communicate with one

DOI: 10.1201/9781003441601-4

another in order to cooperate and work together. Agents in a MAS environment collaborate with one another to find solutions to a variety of issues. The research that has been done on business information systems and enterprise integration has made the MAS paradigm a very appropriate platform for integrative decision support within business information systems [1, 2, 3]. When it comes to cloud computing, security is of the highest significance; yet, as the number of users continues to expand, it is getting more difficult to implement. In other words, cloud computing security is becoming more difficult to implement. The technologies that are now being utilized to have control over the cloud have not been able to scale properly to satisfy the needs of multi-tenancy. [Creative Commons] This is due to the fact that they are based on the user IDs of various users who have donated differing amounts of gratuity [4]. This causes them to have a variety of different levels of contribution. On the other hand, there is a possibility that there would be a very large number of users, which would result in a significant rise in the administrative load that is connected with maintaining the security. In order to provide an environment that is capable of carrying out automated searches for services, the use of resources ontologies is required. In the subject of cloud computing, ontology is put to use in a myriad of diverse settings and contexts [5, 6]. The following are some instances of them to illustrate my point:

- Within the field of cloud computing, intelligent ontology-based registries are used for the purpose of facilitating the dynamic discovery of cloud computing resources across a wide range of cloud computing platforms.
- When integrated with this service, the advantages of ontology may be used by software as a service (SaaS) to provide intelligent personalization via customization.
- Utilizing ontology in combination with role-based access control is one way to facilitate the simplification of the overall architecture of the security system.

4.1.1 Types of Cloud

Enterprises often rent out the cloud's available resources for their own use. There are three recognized categories of cloud service offers, and they are as follows:

1. The term "software as a service" refers to apps that may be accessed from any location over the Internet and provide their complete range of services. These services are made possible by the use of a dispersed network of data centers.
2. Platform-as-a-service refers to distributed development platforms that are used in the process of developing apps, web pages, and services that are intended to operate in cloud-based settings.
3. Infrastructure-as-a-service is a business model in which firms provide the fundamental elements necessary to construct cloud services. These services may be accessed via a variety of cloud hosting providers, such as Amazon's

Elastic Computing Cloud (EC2). They consist of a virtualization layer, database servers, web servers, application servers, server load balancers, firewalls, WAN optimizers, routers, and switches.

4.2 Case Study on Clinical Trials

The primary method through which medical research is carried out in order to evaluate novel drugs, equipment, and other things used for medical reasons is via the use of clinical trials. The data gathered during these clinical trials is of utmost significance to the organizations who are conducting the research. As a consequence of this, the gathering, manipulation, and storage of data must be done with extreme caution, all while adhering to the relevant national and international rules. The usage of ontologies is the primary method for addressing problems that are particular to both languages and domains. When it comes to the organization and structuring of knowledge, the discipline of medicine has made substantial use of taxonomies and ontologies in recent years. It is necessary to have a data integration system that is ontology-based in order to solve the challenges that have been occurring. The structure that is explained further down should be able to meet these requirements.

In today's world, semantic technologies that are constructed on top of ontologies and inferencing are seen as one of the most potentially fruitful pathways for the spread of the Semantic Web. This is because these technologies allow for more precise reasoning. In the subject of information science, a knowledge model known as an ontology is one of the tools that is used. The objective of this approach is to provide an explanation of a topic by making use of the structural and semantic components of the topic. The method that is outlined in this article is geared toward the use of ontologies for a variety of activities; the primary focus, however, is placed on the utilization of a business rules approach in order to facilitate interoperability between business users and information systems. This article is available online at www.information-systems-management.com/. It is feasible for agents to interact with one another and share a common set of concepts about settings, user profiles, commodities, and other aspects of the domain because the MAS environment makes use of ontologies. Using an agent-oriented strategy that is founded on ontologies, the purpose of this study is to demonstrate the integration of different information resources for the purpose of providing decision support in enterprises. Ontologies will serve as the primary focus of attention throughout the integration process. Our research was carried out with the purpose of bridging the gap that exists between business users and intelligent agents. Intelligent agents are a subset of application systems that fall into the category of specialized software that is designed to carry out tasks on behalf of users. The modification of ontologies in MAS was expected to be carried out according to a business rules-based strategy, since this was the intention. Our Decision Support System for Multi-Agent System in Enterprises, also known as DSS-MAS, made use of an ontology that was broken down into a variety of different task and domain ontologies. Because of this, business users were able to change these ontologies in an environment that was pleasant to users and did not need them to have an in-depth understanding of technical concepts. We also proposed that one approach that may be utilized to cut down on operational expenditures is computing done in the cloud. We used one of the commercial clouds in order to accomplish our goals of storing a large amount of data and carrying out a significant amount of Online Analytical Processing (OLAP).

The remaining parts of this work are organized as described in the following. To begin, we will provide an introduction and some history. Next, the following part, is where we provide our case study of an integrated multi-agent environment taken from the industry of medium-sized construction enterprises. Following the introduction of the architecture and the dissection of the ontology, each individual agent that makes up DSS-MAS will be discussed. In the next part, you will get an outline of our strategy for implementing the prototype. In the next part, we will provide a perspective about the use of cloud computing in order to reduce operating expenses. In conclusion, the last part gives some findings as well as some ideas for further study.

4.3 Integrated Multi-Agent Environment

The Decision Support System for Multi-Agent System in Enterprises (DSS-MAS), which is shown in Figure 4.1, is one of the ideas that we propose in this body of work. This article will focus on a case study from the industry of construction firms. The case study will be centered on the commercial environment and

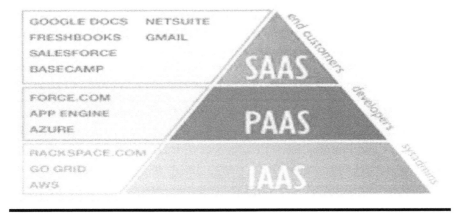

Figure 4.1 Variety of cloud.

Source: https://techstagram.com/2013/02/19/types-of-cloud/

information resources originating from one of the mobile service providers. On the World Wide Web, users have access not only to the Data Mining Decision Support System (DMDSS), also known as the Data Warehouse (DW), but also to a variety of other resources that are in no way associated with the organization. The DSS-MAS infrastructure shares its environment with a number of other systems that perform similar functions.

The overarching goal that DSS-MAS agents strive to achieve is to provide support for the process of decision-making while utilizing the business analytic systems that are already in place within the company and making use of the information that can be gleaned from the environment in which the organization is situated. In order to give assistance for this purpose, DSS-MAS combines a number of agent roles from a variety of sources. Data Mining Agent (DMA), Online Analytical Processing Agent (OLAPA), Information Retrieval Agent (IRA), Knowledge Discovery Agent (KDA), Notifying Agent (NA), and Mobile Agent (MA) are the many agent functions. The primary element of interconnectivity that is used for the representation of domain knowledge, communication between agents, and, most importantly, communication between agents and business users is ontologies. Ontologies are used for these purposes because they are the foundation of ontology-based interconnectivity. Because it is the site where agents perform the information retrieval function in order to achieve the aim of decision making, the World Wide Web is a very important component of an environment. The information that was gathered is contributed to the central knowledge base, and it is also available for inclusion in other studies, such as data mining and data warehousing. In addition, the information may be used to answer questions that are posed by users. After all of the data has been collected from both internal and external sources, it is then subjected to a more in-depth analysis by KDA, with the primary emphasis being focused on inference across a variety of distinct task ontologies. The system has to be aware of its context and take into account the important aspects of the company, which includes taking into account information about the context such as the time, place, and the user's preferences [1]. The business users are the ones who are accountable for recording the preliminary analysis in the ontology, while the agents are the ones who are accountable for the execution and optimization of the process. When the business user is required to take any action, he is notified and given the choice to either take action or alter the rules that control the execution of the agent. This occurs when any action is required of the business user (Figure 4.2).

We provide ontologies as a framework for information exchange between actors (agents and business users) that interact with DSS-MAS in order to make it feasible for these functionalities to be used. This is accomplished via the use of a mediation mechanism known as an ontology. Ontology may be segmented into a variety of separate sub-ontologies [2]. We have developed a higher ontology that we refer to as the Common ontology, and it was named after its intended use. The domain and task ontologies of the Notifying ontology, the Information Retrieval ontology, and the Data Mining and Warehousing ontologies are all combined

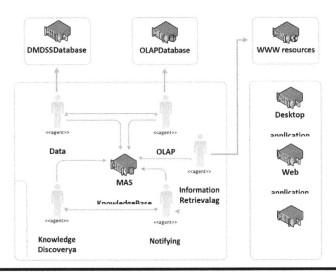

Figure 4.2   Structural design of MAS for decision support system in enterprises.

Source: www.mdpi.com/2227-9717/8/3/312

into one ontology. Both abstract conceptions and reusable dimensions are used by KDA in the fundamental meaning. The scope of the Common ontology is limited to that of abstract notions, and it includes reusable dimensions. Concepts such as notification, information retrieval, data mining, and data warehousing are all examples of things that may be described by task ontologies. The ontology is not only a central repository for the representation of business vocabulary along with all of the restrictions and formal definition of business, but it also consists of dynamic elements in the form of business rules that are used to support operation, advanced analyses, and reuse of existing systems. In other words, the ontology is not only a repository for the formal definition of business but also for the restrictions that are placed on business. In other words, the ontology is not just a repository for business jargon, but it also contains all of the limits and the formal definition of what business is the activities of a construction company of medium size will serve as the foundation for our inquiry, and the marketing and sale of construction services will be the primary focus of our attention during the course of the investigation [3]. Two very different kinds of agents are responsible for dealing with the data storage systems that are in place inside an organization. Online Analytical Processing Agents (OLAPA) and Data Mining Agents (DMA) are both terms that may be used to refer to these agents. Both of them are in charge of different responsibilities, but they are cooperating in order to accomplish the same overarching objective, which is to independently carry out analytical models in either accordance with a predetermined timetable or whenever the situation calls for it [7]. This is the goal that they are working toward. Either the information on the execution is stored in the ontology (according to the wishes of the business user), or another agent who is operating inside the system makes a request for it. On the one hand, the OLAPA is tasked with performing OLAP analyses on behalf of an agent or a business user and reporting its findings back to the requesting entity as well as all other entities that, according to the business policy, should be proactively informed. On the other hand, it is the responsibility of the OLAPA to carry out OLAP analyses on behalf of an agent or a business user [8]. On the other hand, it is OLAPA's duty to conduct research of this kind on behalf of any and all other organizations that are pertinent. After each execution, OLAPA will provide a report for the business user based on the results that were observed. This is only one of the many things that OLAPA is still capable of doing beyond this [5]. In the event that the outcomes of an earlier test and the current one are quite dissimilar to one another, further testing is carried out in order to determine the cause of the gap in outcomes. Either digging more into the hierarchies or climbing higher up the tiers is a viable option for accomplishing this goal.

Since the information is stored in ontology, we provide business users the power to alter the behavior of agents by merely updating the ontology via the utilization of a simple graphical user interface. This is possible because we have captured the information in ontology. All of the logical restrictions that are outlined in the ontology have been included into the design of this interface [9–11]. It also does not let users enter wrong inputs, and perhaps most crucially, it does not need users to have any kind of technical expertise in order to utilize it. It is a well-known fact that only around twenty percent of the information that may be included in structured data that is stored in relational databases may be accessed and put to use in a company's business intelligence system. This percentage is based on the broad consensus of industry experts [2, 12]. The remaining eighty percent of the material is either totally unstructured or just moderately arranged in the documents. This organization ranges from slight to full. Because of this, the DSS-MAS system includes something called the Information Retrieval Agent (IRA), which is designed to get information and data mostly from the World Wide Web. The functions carried out by the IRA may be classified into the following three categories:

- Identification of newly discovered construction enterprises online
- An examination of the services provided by several different building businesses
- Completing the Data Warehouse using information retrieved from the Internet

Evaluations are conducted on every Internet construction company that has just come to light. IRA visits a number of different construction companies in order to build a list of the services offered together with their prices in the present market. After that, these details are filed away in the information retrieval ontology, where the Knowledge Discovery Agent will be able to retrieve them at a later time for the purpose of more knowledge extraction (KDA). Found services are used for a wide range of objectives, including but not limited to the identification of newly emerging market trends, the facilitation of price comparisons between competitors, the authorization of possible inclusion in an organization's sales program, and many more.

The IRA is responsible for a number of things, one of which is the addition of information that can be found online to the analyses that are done in the Data Warehouse. When a business user is doing an OLAP analysis, the only information he works with relates to the firm itself and is considered confidential. However, before judgments can be made, other resources, such as news about the suppliers and rivals, views about certain items and organizations, and so on, need to be studied as well. This is necessary before decisions can be made. The IRA will then use this information to search across a range of different web sites. In order to get this information, the dimension data included inside the Data Warehouse's dimensional schema are traversed (via their respective hierarchies and levels) (news archives, forums, stock changes, Google trends etc.). When customers access OLAP reports, the data from the Internet is also presented to them in accordance with the dimensions that are limited to their needs. Knowledge Discovery Agent (KDA) is a very vital part of DSS-MAS since it not only mediates derived discoveries to Notification but also consolidates all of the results from Information Retrieval, Data Mining, and Warehousing. This makes it one of the most important parts of the system. In order for businesses to get the most of their usage of inference capabilities across a wide variety of ontologies, it is very necessary for them to have established business rules. Even if ontology may include business concepts, it is still necessary for these ideas to be linked to one another in order for the information to be usable. As a standard practice, business users, as opposed to technical users, are the ones who are responsible for the creation of business rules. In addition, business rules inside firms have a propensity to change often; as a consequence, we designed an architecture (see Figure 4.3) for managing business rules in order to accommodate this tendency.

As can be seen in Figure 4.1, the Notifying Agent (NA) acts as a gateway or interface to the DSS-MAS for any and all business users and applications that are reachable from the outside world. The basic role of NA is the conveyance of information, which may be performed by just delivering the proper material at the appropriate timing to the suitable customers. All of the information that is currently available about notifications is saved inside the Notifying ontology. Every user has their very own context described inside this ontology, in addition to their position within the company in terms of two distinct dimensions: organizational unit (such as marketing, sales, or human resources), and decision-making level (e.g., CEO, CIO, CFO, etc.). As a result of this circumstance, the guidelines for the sending of a wide range of various kinds of communications have been outlined in more detail. The many different types of messages range from simple notifications to more important cautions and alerts of a crucial nature.

4.4 Related Work and Literature Review

Ontology is characterized as the unequivocal conventional particular of conceptualization [13]. Ontologies are totally the mainstay of a few cloud applications requiring explicit space information [14]. In a cloud climate, distinguishing and sorting cloud administrations in reality could be testing since cloud administrations are furnished at different help levels with process information, business rationale, and equipment capacities [15]. Metaphysics gives coordinated rules of suggestions, each with obviously specified rules that the machine can comprehend, subsequently adding to machine insight [16]. The cloud ontology gives meta-data about information semantics, covering cloud models and their connections [17]. A metaphysics addresses area information; the philosophy engineer makes ontology classes by making graphical models. This is on the grounds that models are said to have clear semantics. In light of the aforementioned, ontology-based space information can make unambiguous proper standards to such an extent that models can be expressive and deciphered by the two machines and people [18]. Philosophy has been applied to numerous regions since the approach of distributed computing, going about as the missing connection among people and machines to accommodate the heterogeneous idea of the cloud coming about because of the absence of standard and administration structure.

Ontologies are key apparatuses for semantic online application(s) [19]; consequently, their assessments are vital for upgrading their (semantic) quality. Most philosophy specialists would prefer to have a particular ontology instead of an overall metaphysics. This is on the grounds that a decent quality secluded metaphysics will advance reusability [20]. The exploration work done by [21] fostered a design that utilizes double center philosophy parts, in particular, the List and Business Cycle ontology, with the limit with regards to augmentation through the expansion of explicit area ontologies. The index metaphysics investigates Universal Business Language (UBL), while the Business Cycle Ontology utilizes different relevant business measurements. The business interaction consolidates decides that different semantic analyzers for business practices can comprehend. The exhibition of metaphysics is supposed to be productive in light of the profundity chose; in the event that the profundity is exceptionally high, it suggests that the information move will be exceptionally definite. In any case, information move and test will be shallow. Then, there will be no competitive edge and the framework will be lost [22]. The creators of the Overall Information Security Guideline (GDPR) structure fostered an engineering in view of the consequences of the DAPRECO project. A result of GDPR contains not just lawful directions and thoughts got inside the legitimate climate, however semantic arrangements in view of commitments, consents, and restrictions [23]. The MEASUR's philosophy was created as a model that offers a non-dynamic variant of the undertaking designs. This structure is being applied to different situations, and it has answered well by giving verification of solidarity. The creators proposed a framework that upheld an ontological judgment framework to help partners in tolerating such resolutions under electronic administration strategies [24]. The creators of [25] proposed a cycle philosophy-based way to deal with semantic vagueness by giving a way to catch rich semantic data dwelling in business processes, which can be accomplished by utilizing space-explicit ontologies. The creators of [26] introduced a structure comprised of a rundown of standards and a conventional consistence checking approach in light of cycle execution. The creators of [27] proposed a semantic system in light of an Internet of Things in Business Cycles Philosophy (IoT-BCP) semantic model. The creators of [28] made a philosophy with the capacity to portray connections among different partners engaged with the cloud climate. The methodology performs security evaluation according to various clients' perspectives. The creators of [29] introduced a security design that acts as a base for depicting the difficulties connected with security prerequisites. In another work, the creators [30] displayed their ITAOFIR (IT Asset Ontology for Information Risk) metaphysics as a powerful portrayal of IT resources substance and hazard. In the interim, the creators of [31] constructed an unmistakable portrayal in the midst of view of conventions and models, and they utilized semantic business vocabularies combined with rules in light of likeness measures. Express displaying and planning of vocabularies in the consistence system climate will facilitate the pressure space specialists experience while evaluating for the ampleness of explicit guidelines [32].

The work in [33] proposed a semantic-based help portrayal and disclosure outline work, which utilizes a multi-specialist approach and metaphysics with a model for cloud administration depiction and revelation in the distributed computing space. A system [34] was conceptual in nature and was utilized for Proceeded with Cycle Reviewing (CA) depending on space ontologies.

The creators of [35] fostered a thinking system that works on the goal of likeness clashes between cloud administrations through a distributed computing metaphysics.

According to [36], the justification behind including ontologies in distributed computing is because of its capacity to diminish search time, fast revelation of assets, and precise outcomes. In [37], the authors proposed a methodology that could normalize security data to accomplish new comprehension. The methodology further offer the executives aggregate and in fact dependable choice options. The creators needed to make a total bundle of IT with security ontologies that have directed administration structures in light of the ISO 27002 norm. Their structure was approved with a model, systems, and curios utilizing trained professionals and clients from small organizations.

An ontology-based framework administration disclosure and determination model is recommended that indicates pragmatic and non-viable necessities [38]. The authors applied ontology to work on the viability and precision of the model. The proposed model helped the shoppers in searching and choosing the most

	Cloud Services Discovery and Selection
[40] Joshi et al. (2020)	"Cloud Security comparator system"
[41] Afgan et al. (2018)	"CloudLaunch: Discover and deploy cloud applications"
[15] Alfazi et al. (2015)	"Ontology-Based Automatic Cloud Service Categorization for Enhancing Cloud Service Discovery"
[42] Ali et al. (2018)	"Cloud Service Discovery and Extraction: A Critical Review and Direction for Future Research"
[43] Androcec et al. (2012)	"Cloud Computing Ontologies: A systematic review"
[44] Mordi & Garg (2019)	"A QoS-based approach for cloud-service matchmaking, selection and composition using the "An MCDM method for cloud service selection using a Markov chain and the best-worst method. Knowledge Based System"
[45] Sbodio et al. (2010)	"Discovering Semantic Web services using SPARQL and intelligent agents. Web Semantics"
[46] DiMartino et al. (2016)	"Cloud services composition through cloud patterns: a semantic-based approach" Cloud Services Description and Selection
[47] Nawaz et al. (2019)	"Service description languages in cloud computing: state-of-the-art and research issues"
[48] Chen and Yang, 2020	"Ontology for cloud manufacturing based Product Lifecycle Management"
[49] Greenwell et al. (2016)	"Cloud energy saving case-based reasoning agent" "ManuService ontology: a product data model for service-oriented business interactions in a cloud manufacturing environment"
[50] Brogi et al. (2019)	"A Task Orientated Requirements Ontology for Cloud Computing Services" Cloud Security and Compliance Ontology

appropriate merchant with a high degree of exactness. The creators of [39] introduced a model to upgrade the number of inhabitants in a consistence philosophy by utilizing data separated from a current Governance Risk Compliance (GRC). The proposed work was designed to improve semantic interoperability and reduce the intricacy and the handicapped capabilities.

4.5 Delegation of Authority

In this algorithmic depth guide, we discuss how authority may be delegated over a certain resource. Specifically, we focus on the algorithmic aspects of this process. An instance of each of these three entities is delivered to the system whenever a request is made to a system for a delegate to carry out a job. These requests may be made in a variety of ways. The verification of the delegator's authorization and privileges in their capacity as a delegator kicks off the processing of delegation requests at line 1, which is the first step in the delegation process. It begins with the establishment of a link to the delegator's local repository of policies, which the delegator is responsible for maintaining given that the delegator has sufficient delegation permissions (see line 2). Line 3: at this stage in the process, it is required to distinguish between the kinds of delegators (i.e., owner and delegate) in order to design the suitable policy, which may either be a trusted policy or a delegated policy. The construction of the appropriate policy depends on this distinction. In line 4, a consideration is given to the sort of topic delegator that is being looked at. In the event that the delegator is also the owner of the resource that serves as the focal point of the policy, then the parameters of the trusted policy have already been defined. The user has the ability to establish the maximum number of delegates that may be used on the target resource. This can be done by utilizing the property of delegation level (line 5), which is normally defined by the owner of the target resource. At line 6, the proprietor's private key is put to use in order to generate a digital signature for the proprietor's identity; this signature is then saved within the characteristics of the trusted policy. In the event that the delegator is not also the owner of the resource, the resource's delegation level may have to be decreased in order to make room for the newly imposed constraints (line 7–8). If the level of delegation (i.e., the maximum level designated by the owner) exceeds a preset threshold (i.e., the maximum level established by the owner), then attempts to delegate will not be permitted. This is because the owner has the ability to decide the maximum level of delegation (line 19). It is also possible to modify delegation rules so that they reflect the planned activity (such as reading, writing, etc.) that is to be carried out. This is done by developing a policy rule in accordance with the access right, i.e., the intended action (line 10–18).

Delegation of Authority (Subject–Delegator, Subject–Delegate, Object–Resource, Action), an Algorithm

1. Position of power: Check the delegate's authority (the subject delegate, the object resource, and the action).
2. Determine if the authority in question is legitimate.
3. Establish a link with the subject delegator's local data base.
4. If the subject delegator also serves as the owner, then the subject delegator also serves as the owner.
5. Set delegation level: /e.g. default value is '5'.

6. Ensure that you have a trustworthy insurance coverage by having the owner sign anything that identifies them.
7. Others are responsible for developing delegated policy.
8. Delegation level = Delegation level–1.
9. In the event that the delegation level is greater than zero, the value 10 applies.
10. In the event that the delegation level is more than zero, then
11. Develop a brand-new regulation for the policy that will be applicable to the individual who will be the topic delegatee.
12. To specify the new policy, provide the policy rule as well as the specifications for the delegation level.
13. If the subject delegator already has a policy set for the object resource, then the subject delegator will do the following:
14. Incorporate a new policy into the set of policies that is already in effect.
15. Else
16. Create a whole new set of policy guidelines.
17. Include the policy in the overall collection of policies; finish if the following:
18. A shop policy was entered into the database, which the subject delegator is able to read locally.
19. Create instance relations using subject delegator, subject delegatee, object resource, and policy set.
20. If the object resource has already reached the maximum number of delegations allowed, abort the operation.
21. Else not a valid delegator.

After the inclusion of a delegate policy rule and the adjustment of the resource delegation level, the process of developing policies is complete (line 12). To begin, the system searches the delegator's repository for a policy set that is specific to the resource to which they want to offer access authorization. This ensures that no other policies exist to conflict with the desired access authorization (line 13). If the delegator already has a policy in place, the new policy will be added to the one that is currently in place (line 14). In such a scenario, a brand-new set of guidelines is crafted for the delegator, and the policy in issue is included into the brand-new set of guidelines (lines 15–16). The delegation process is created when the delegation policy is established and then saved in the repository of the delegator. This is followed by the instantiation of the appropriate ontological classes (delegator, delegatee, delegated resource, and policy set) as well as the relationships that are associated with them. This takes place throughout the process of establishing the delegation policy (line 17–18).

4.6 Result and Discussion

In order to facilitate the delegation of access control in cloud-based scenarios, it is necessary to classify cloud entities in accordance with the roles that they play and the kinds of services that they provide. This is done so that users will have an easier time managing the rights assigned to them. This categorization was developed with the intention of facilitating the management of delegation across all three tiers of cloud service (i.e., IaaS, PaaS, and SaaS), as well as the provision of an infrastructure for the administration of policies across all three levels. This categorization was developed with the intention of facilitating the management of delegation across all three tiers of cloud service. These are the goals that are going to be accomplished as a direct consequence of using this categorization system. As a direct result of this, there are primarily three types of organizations that are accountable for the administration of cloud resources. These organizations are as follows: i refers to the cloud provider, which might be a company like Google; ii refers to cloud service providers like Gmail and Google Drive; and iii refers to users, or renters. Cloud service providers (also known as CSPs) are dependent on cloud providers for their infrastructure requirements, which may include servers, storage, and other components. In a manner fairly similarly to this, cloud service providers offer their clients a diverse selection of platforms, services, and apps to choose from. The real people who are using the cloud services, known as tenants, have the capacity to collaborate with other users in the management of shared resources (for example, individuals or departments inside the business). This takes us to the conclusion of our discussion.

If these entities are going to be in a position to provide a decentralized delegation of authority, then they will need to have distributed local repositories in which they are able to store their policies. They will then be able to manage their resources on their own thanks to this. This distribution is being done with the intention of providing a method for decentralizing the power in order to lessen the burden that comes with the administration of policies by a single body. The following information may be found in Figure 4.3, which depicts the flow of delegation and the maintenance of policies inside the cloud entities. This diagram also includes the following components.

At the beginning of the delegation process, the cloud provider (CP) may delegate some of its resources to the cloud service providers (CSPs) by storing the rules governing those CSPs in its own local repository. This is known as the first layer of the delegation process. One may consider this an example of delegating resource responsibility. This repository contains a variety of shared resources, and the CP is liable for the maintenance of policy sets connected to each of these shared resources. Each policy set is composed of the policies—also called access policies or administrative policies, depending on the context—of all of the organizations who collaborate on the management of the resource in question. The term "policies" may also be used to refer to these stipulations in their simplest form.

The entities that make up the second layer are responsible for managing access rights on resources (for example, the services that are owned by the CSPs or the resources that have been delegated by the CP) by maintaining policies in the local repository that is managed by the CSPs. In a manner analogous to this, the entities that make up the second layer are responsible for managing access rights on resources. Cloud service providers, have the ability to delegate resources to either other cloud service providers (on the same level, as in the case of a federated cloud scenario) or to tenants of the cloud. The upkeep of policy sets is what makes this possibility conceivable (i.e., third-level organizations).

4.7 Future Work

The tenants who make up the third tier are the ones who are responsible for the administration of the resources that the CSPs have allocated to them. This accountability comes from the fact that they are the ones who make up the third layer. In turn, the CSPs have the freedom to further allocate resources to other tenants by maintaining their own rules, given that the policies that have been delegated to them allow them to do so. This is granted that the CSPs are allowed to do so by the policies that have been assigned to them.

Entities (at each level of delegation) are permitted to use the same space to store their policies even if the CP is the one who is responsible for maintaining and sharing the storage area. This is the case since the CP is the one who first created the storage area. In spite of the fact that the CP is the one who shares the storage space, this is still the situation. On the other hand, if these entities so choose, they

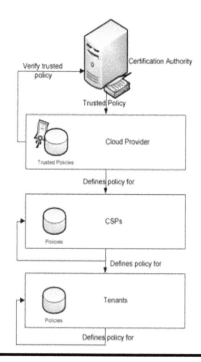

Figure 4.3 Implementation of policies within cloud entities using entrustment.

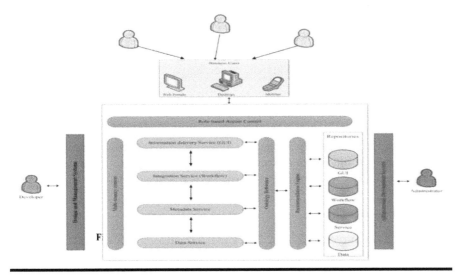

Figure 4.4   Cloud services ontology with multi-agent ecosystems.

are free to independently administer their own local repositories. This privilege is available to them. Even though the repositories are administered in a decentralized fashion, the system is still able to link all of the entities by using a conventional delegation method. This is possible despite the fact that the repository management is decentralized. This is feasible as a result of the management practices followed by the repositories. Therefore, adhering to the standard delegation protocol makes it possible to do a straightforward verification of the delegator's authority in response to an access request made at any level by the entities.

To prevent the forging of the delegators' identities, the workflow created by the delegation process must be trusted. The owner of the resources digitally signs its policies, which are referred to as trusted policies, in order to build this level of confidence. Each access request to a resource must be authenticated using a trusted policy, which serves as a dependable way for doing so. To do so, the delegation process must originate from a trusted policy signed by the resource's owner.

4.8 Proposed Framework

The proposed framework will have four layers, as follows:

Data Layer

Different groups in a domain create ontology systems with numerous data sources. Integrating ontology refers to the process of building a more comprehensive ontology on top of an already existing one, in order to address heterogeneity difficulties. Using a tree structure, the ontology will be the value 1. The ontology will serve as a guide for the design of data layers. The template is found and modified using ontology information after a domain search for ontology.

Service Layer

There are two types of services: basic and complex. An atomic service performs basic actions, but a composite service is composed of many atomic services linked together to perform more complicated functions. Every service has its own set of rules and regulations, and ontology is used to do complex tasks [51].

Business Process Layer

With its services and participants, this layer is capable of achieving complicated business tasks and workflows, which include activities and reflect the flow of information in a business process. Tenants may use keywords to search a workflow repository and have access to the applicable workflows based on their specific needs and interests. Customization revolves on business domain knowledge and is based on a multi-layered workflow that incorporates a number of stages or transformations generated from template objects [52].

User Interface Layer

There are several ways to construct a user interface ontology that will allow you to find and reason about various aspects of user interfaces. To include user interface categorization information, the ontology should be restructured. Among the sorts of information available are data gathering and representation, command and control, monitoring, and hybrid. Change and adjust the look and feel of the user interface, including adding or removing icons, fonts, and other concerns. This is the simplest method of user interface modification [53].

4.9 Conclusion

In this chapter, we built an enforcement mechanism for XACML delegations based on an ontological model of the delegation process. This model served as the foundation for our work. In densely populated environments such as the cloud, this indicates that the processes of delegating, confirming, and revoking authorization may be managed in a way that is more scalable. Intelligent behavior on the part of both the Multi-Agent System as a whole and its individual components is what sets Multi-Agent Systems apart from other types of distributed systems (Figure 4.4). There has been an increase in the need for technological solutions that are compatible with the Multi-Agent Systems (MAS) paradigm, which is becoming more prevalent in the management of larger and more intricate scenarios. MASs are not only versatile and intricate in terms of agent interaction and organization, but they also exhibit a wide variety of structures. A further advantage of using a MAS is the ability to work with groups of agents. As a result of this, it functions as an effective metaphor for visualizing and outlining a diverse variety of software applications. On the other side, Multi-Agent Systems make it easier for a variety of frameworks to operate together. It is a goal to "agentify" the heterogeneous segments, which means to wrap these segments in an operator layer that enables them to communicate with one another using a common agent communication language. Another way to say this is that the "agentification" of the heterogeneous segments is the goal.

References

1. Mell, P.; Grance, T. The NIST definition of cloud computing. Available online: http://faculty.winthrop.edu/domanm/csci411/Handouts/NIST.pdf (accessed on 29 October 2021).
2. Odun-Ayo, I.; Misra, S.; Omoregbe, N.; Onibere, E.; Bulama, Y.; Damasevic̆ius, R. Cloud-based security driven human resource management system. In Proceedings of the 20th International Conference of the Catalan Association for Artificial Intelligence, Deltebre, Terres de l'Ebre, 25–27 October 2017.
3. Al-Sayed, M.M.; Hassan, H.A.; Omara, F.A. Towards evaluation of cloud ontologies. J. Parallel Distrib. Comput. 2019, 126, 82–106.
4. Schmidt, E. Conversation with Eric Schmidt hosted by Danny Sullivan. Search Engine Strategies Conference, 2006. Available online: www.google.com/press/podium/ses2006.html (accessed on 29 October 2021).
5. Zhang, Q.; Cheng, L.; Boutaba, R. Cloud computing: State-of-the-art and research challenges. J. Internet Serv. Appl. 2010, 1, 7–18.
6. Qian, L.; Luo, Z.; Du, Y.; Guo, L. Cloud computing: An overview. Available online: https://link.springer.com/chapter/10.1007/978-3-642-10665-1_63#citeas (accessed on 29 October 2021).
7. Da Silva, F.S.; Nascimento, M.H.R. Major challenges facing cloud migration. J. Eng. Technol. Ind. Appl. 2020, 6, 59–65.
8. Buzys, R.; Maskeliunas, R.; Damaševic̆ius, R.; Sidekerskiene, T.; Woźniak, M.; Wei, W. Cloudification of virtual reality gliding simulation game. Information 2018, 9, 293.
9. Reimerink, A.A.; Helver, M. Security and compliance ontology for cloud service agreements. Int. J. Cloud Comput. Database Manag. 2020, 1, 18–23.
10. Zhu, J. Cloud computing technologies and applications. Available online: https://link.springer.com/chapter/10.1007/978-1-4419-6524-0_2 (accessed on 29 October 2021).
11. Dillon, T.; Wu, C.; Chang, E. Cloud computing: Issues and challenges. In Proceedings of the 2010 24th IEEE International Conference on Advanced Information Networking and Applications, Perth, 20–23 April 2010.
12. Danevic̆ius, E.; Maskeliunas, R.; Damaševic̆ius, R.; Połap, D.; Woźniak, M. A soft body physics simulator with computational offloading to the cloud. Information 2018, 9, 318.

13. Gruber, T. "What is ontology?" Encyclopedia of Database Systems. Available online: https://link.springer.com/referenceworkentry/10.1007%2F978-0-387-39940-9_1318 (accessed on 29 October 2021).

14. Flahive, A.; Taniar, D.; Rahayu, W. Ontology as a service (OaaS): A case for sub-ontology merging on the cloud. J. Supercomput. 2011, 65, 1–32.

15. Alfazi, A.; Sheng, Q.Z.; Qin, Y.; Noor, T.H. Ontology-based automatic cloud service categorization for enhancing cloud service discovery. In Proceedings of the 2015 IEEE 19th International Enterprise Distributed Object Computing Conference, Adelaide, 21–25 September 2015.

16. Tankelevičiene, L.; Damaševičius, R. Towards the development of genuine intelligent ontology-based e-learning systems. In Proceedings of the IEEE International Conference on Intelligent Systems, Xiamen, 29–31 October 2010, pp. 79–84.

17. Kang, J.; Sim, K.M. Ontology and search engine for cloud computing. In Proceedings of the International Conference on System Science and Engineering, Yichang, Hubei, 12–14 November 2010, pp. 276–281.

18. Hinkelmann, K.; Laurenzi, E.; Martin, A.; Thönssen, B. Ontology-based metamodeling. Stud. Syst. Decis. Control 2018, 141, 177–194.

19. Sowunmi, O.Y.; Misra, S.; Omoregbe, N.; Damasevicius, R.; Maskeliunas, R. A semantic web-based framework for information retrieval in E-learning systems. In International Conference on Recent Developments in Science, Engineering and Technology. Cham: Springer, 2018, pp. 96–106.

20. Baliyan, N.; Verma, A. Recent advances in the evaluation of ontology quality. Available online: www.igi-global.com/chapter/recent-advances-in-the-evaluation-of-ontology-quality/215071 (accessed on 29 October 2021).

21. Deng, Q.; Gönül, S.; Kabak, Y.; Gessa, N.; Glachs, D.; Gigante-Valencia, F.; Thoben, K.D. An ontology framework for multisided platform interoperability. In Enterprise Interoperability VIII. Cham: Springer, 2019, pp. 433–443.

22. Gábor, A.; Ko, A.; Szabó, Z.; Fehér, P. Corporate knowledge discovery and organizational learning: The role, importance, and application of semantic business process management—The ProKEX case. In Knowledge Management and Organizational Learning. Cham: Springer, 2016, pp. 1–31.

23. Bartolini, C.; Calabró, A.; Marchetti, E. GDPR and business processes. In Proceedings of the 2nd International Conference on Applications of Intelligent Systems, New York, NY, 7–9 January 2019.

24. Di Martino, B.; Marino, A.; Rak, M.; Pariso, P. Optimization and validation of e-government business processes with support of semantic techniques. Available online: https://link.springer.com/chapter/10.1007/978-3-030-22354-0_76#citeas (accessed on 29 October 2021).

25. Fan, S.; Hua, Z.; Storey, V.C.; Zhao, J.L. A process ontology based approach to easing semantic ambiguity in business process modeling. Data Knowl. Eng. 2016, 102, 57–77.

26. Hashmi, M.; Governatori, G.; Wynn, M.T. Normative requirements for regulatory compliance: An abstract formal framework. Inf. Syst. Front. 2015, 18, 429–455.

27. Suri, K.; Gaaloul, W.; Cuccuru, A.; Gerard, S. Semantic framework for internet of things-aware business process development. In Proceedings of the 2017 IEEE 26th International Conference on Enabling Technologies: Infrastructure for Collaborative Enterprises (WETICE), Poznan, 21–23 June 2017.

28. Manzoor, S.; Vateva-Gurova, T.; Trapero, R.; Suri, N. Threat modeling the cloud: An ontology based approach. Curr. Top. Behav. Neurosci. 2019, 11398, 61–72.
29. Arogundade, O.T.; Jin, Z.; Yang, X. Towards ontological approach to eliciting risk-based security requirements. Int. J. Inf. Comput. Secur. 2014, 6, 143.
30. Adesemowo, A.K.; von Solms, R.; Botha, R.A. ITAOFIR: IT asset ontology for information risk in knowledge economy and beyond. In Communications in Computer and Information Science (Global Security, Safety and Sustainability-The Security Challenges of the Connected World); Jahankhani, H., Carlile, A., Emm, D., Hosseinian-Far, A., Brown, G., Sexton, G., Jamal, A., Eds., Volume 630. London: Springer International Publishing, 2017, pp. 173–187.
31. Sunkle, S.; Kholkar, D.; Kulkarni, V. Toward better mapping between regulations and operational details of enterprises using vocabularies and semantic similarity. Complex Syst. Inform. Modeling Q. 2016, 5, 39–60.
32. Mustapha, A.M.; Arogundade, O.T.; Misra, S.; Damasevicius, R.; Maskeliunas, R. A systematic literature review on compliance requirements management of business processes. Int. J. Syst. Assur. Eng. Manag. 2020, 11, 561–576.
33. Parhi, M.; Pattanayak, B.K.; Patra, M.R. A multi-agent-based framework for cloud service description and discovery using ontology. Intell. Comput. Commun. Dev. 2014, 308, 337–348.
34. Subhani, N.; Kent, R.D. Continuous process auditing (CPA): An audit rule ontology based approach to audit-as-a-service. In Proceedings of the 2015 Annual IEEE Systems Conference (SysCon) Proceedings, Vancouver, BC, 13–16 April 2015.
35. Parhi, M.; Pattanayak, B.K.; Patra, M.R. A multi-agent-based framework for cloud service discovery and selection using ontology. Serv. Oriented Comput. Appl. 2017, 12, 137–154.
36. Ageed, Z.S.; Ibrahim, R.K.; Sadeeq, M.A.M. Unified ontology implementation of cloud computing for distributed systems. Curr. J. Appl. Sci. Technol. 2020, 39, 82–97.
37. Fenz, S.; Neubauer, T. Ontology-based information security compliance determination and control selection on the example of ISO 27002. Inf. Comput. Secur. 2018, 26, 551–567.
38. Parhi, M.; Pattanayak, B.K.; Patra, M.R. An ontology-based cloud infrastructure service discovery and selection system. Int. J. Grid Util. Comput. 2018, 9, 108.
39. Cheng, D.C.; Lim-Cheng, N.R. An ontology based framework to support multi-standard compliance for an enterprise. In Proceedings of the International Conference on Research and Innovation in Information Systems (ICRIIS), Langkawi, 16–17 July 2017.
40. Joshi, K.P.; Elluri, L.; Nagar, A. An integrated knowledge graph to automate cloud data compliance. IEEE Access 2020, 8, 148541–148555.
41. Afgan, E.; Lonie, A.; Taylor, J.; Goonasekera, N. CloudLaunch: Discover and deploy cloud applications. Future Gener. Comput. Syst. 2018, 94, 802–810.
42. Ali, A.; Shamsuddin, S.M.; Eassa, F.E.; Mohammed, F. Cloud service discovery and extraction: A critical review and direction for future research. Available online: https://link.springer.com/chapter/10.1007/978-3-319-99007-1_28#citeas (accessed on 29 October 2021).
43. Androcec, D.; Vrcek, N.; Seva, J. Cloud computing ontologies: A systematic review. In Proceedings of the Third International Conference on Models and Ontology-based Design of Protocols, Architectures and Services Cloud, Chamonix/Mont Blanc, 29 April–4 May 2012, pp. 9–14.

44. Modi, K.J.; Garg, S. A QoS-based approach for cloud-service matchmaking, selection and composition using the Semantic Web. J. Syst. Inf. Technol. 2019, 21, 63–89.
45. Sbodio, M.L.; Martin, D.; Moulin, C. Discovering semantic web services using SPARQL and intelligent agents. J. Web Semant. 2010, 8, 310–328.
46. Di Martino, B.; Cretella, G.; Esposito, A. Cloud services composition through cloud patterns: A semantic-based approach. Soft Comput. 2016, 21, 4557–4570.
47. Nawaz, F.; Mohsin, A.; Janjua, N.K. Service description languages in cloud computing: State-of-the-art and research issues. Serv. Oriented Comput. Appl. 2019, 13, 109–125.
48. Yang, S.C.S. A web services, ontology and big data analysis technology-based cloud case-based reasoning agent for energy conservation of sustainability science. Appl. Sci. 2020, 10, 1387.
49. Greenwell, R.; Liu, X.; Chalmers, K.; Pahl, C. Task orientated requirements ontology for cloud computing services. Available online: www.scitepress.org/papers/2016/57523/57523.pdf (accessed on 29 October 2021).
50. Brogi, A.; Ferrari, G.L.; Forti, S. Secure cloud-edge deployments, with trust. Future Gener. Comput. Syst. 2019, 102, 775–788.
51. El-Gazzar, R.; Hustad, E.; Olsen, D.H. Understanding cloud computing adoption issues: A Delphi study approach. J. Syst. Softw. 2016, 118, 64–84.
52. Opara-Martins, J.; Sahandi, R.; Tian, F. Critical analysis of vendor lock-in and its impact on cloud computing migration: A business perspective. J. Cloud Comput. Adv. Syst. Appl. 2016, 5, 1–18.
53. Odun-Ayo, I.; Geteloma, V.; Misra, S.; Ahuja, R.; Damasevicius, R. Systematic mapping study of utility-driven platforms for clouds. Proc. Int. Conf. Emerg. Trends Inf. Technol. 2020, 762–774.

Chapter 5

Applicability of Artificial Intelligence for Social Development in Rural and Urban Sectors

Reeti Raj and Sambaditya Raj

5.1 Introduction

Artificial intelligence (AI) refers to a group of algorithmic computer capabilities that can carry out tasks that would normally be performed by humans in a variety of contexts. AI stands for dynamic machine intelligence, which includes, among other things, social intelligence (emotive computing and sentiment analysis), perception (computer vision and speech recognition), whole language processing (chatbots and data mining), and facial recognition (computer vision). The orders that tell computers what to perform, which may be unbiased strings of directives, are the real lines of code that enable AI products. AI has an impact on the developed world and on people's daily life. The majority of companies, NGOs, and the government use AI in their operations, their goods, and in industries like healthcare, education, economics, and agriculture [1].

Machine learning, computer vision, knowledge representation, expert systems, audio processing, and natural language processing are the core artificial intelligence technologies. A lot of research is being done now in the field of artificial intelligence, and it is showing promise. Healthcare, robotics, the military, agriculture, retail, manufacturing, game-playing, the arts, banking and finance, automobiles, energy, and advertising are some of the notable application fields of artificial intelligence. There is great opportunity potential of artificial intelligence in the areas of social work and social development [2].

The emergence of these highly automated technologies has sparked interest in studying how digital decision-making might function to concentrate human bias in the academic, industrial, and government sectors. This appeal for the technology industry and computer and data science programmes to include ethical and social justice-centred design is a big potential for social work. Social work is well positioned to interact across disciplines to support the development of meaningful algorithmically improved policy and practice at all levels since it is a values-centred profession with a strong code of ethics. Social workers are especially qualified to support algorithmic product developers as they experimentally assess the efficacy of their algorithms because of social work's basic ideals of social justice, honesty, and the importance of relationships [2, 3].

For its implementation, artificial intelligence can be framed in various ways based on its validation and implications. It can be used in general in diversified ecological conditions for developing an understanding and connecting with human intelligence. Figure 5.1 illustrates the knowledge of both narrow and general artificial intelligences in executing various tasks for enhancing human intelligence and enable development in the urban and rural society [4].

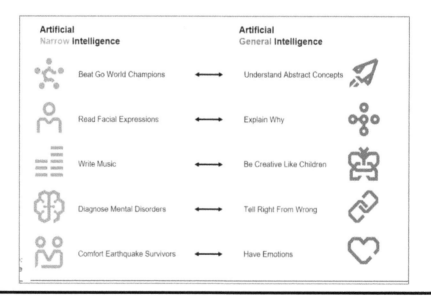

Figure 5.1   Narrow AI vs general AI.

Source: Accenture

5.2 Literature Review

With India's rapid growth in the global economy, the artificial intelligence is at stake with the potential to transform its approach by adopting new and emerging technology. Some recent studies emphasize the requirement of artificial intelligence tools and their applicability in the social development both in the urban and rural sectors.

In its assessment report 2018, NITI Aayog critically examines that though the economy is fast growing, artificial intelligence is at stake in a highly populated country like India. On one side the study reports the approach to identify sectors and the potential in adopting and innovating artificial intelligence in various fields. For this the government needs to play a principal role and the willingness for developing a roadmap and ensuring sustainable and scalable solutions through a national strategy for sustainable development.

In the research paper, Goldkind explains the possibility to infuse artificial intelligence in social development practices to study the aspects of human functioning. The advent of automated tools is in demand in various fields, namely education, industry, and the government sectors, to observe the utility of digital decision making to concentrate human behaviour as experimented and applied by faculty and students in their field of practice to develop their knowledge and skills.

Focusing on the sustainable development goals and emphasizing sustainable rural development in India, Mankar in his research paper discusses the importance of artificial intelligence and its impact on adapting the concept of turning villages, towns, and cities into smart villages, smart town, and smart cities. Their study reveals how manual labour can be transformed to artificial intelligence by the use of technology, communications, intelligence, etc. Because technological development and digitization is considered to contribute to changing the society, for sustainable rural development there is a need to incorporate technology in the procedures, products, and services in the fields of healthcare, education, agriculture, or economy.

In his research paper, Jain explores the increased applicability of artificial intelligence (AI) enabled tools for proficient and effective practice among employees in several social development organizations. Emphasizing the unified theory of acceptance and use of technology (UTAUT), they analyzed the impact of AI enabled tools in their work process and performance. For this study, the collected data were analyzed using partial least square (PLS) with a two-step model, measurement, and structural model of assessment. The results revealed were positive, highlighting significant effects of AI aversion in the relationship between their performance expectancy and use of technology. Thus, it is observed that there is an ardent need for adopting AI enabled tools in task execution and organizations also need to address the employees' concern on AI.

Eminent scholars and governmental departments and organizations explain that:

S. No.	Explanation	Scholars and Organizations
1.	The government needs to develop a roadmap for effective application of AI.	NITI Aayog (2018)
2.	AI can perform humanlike functions across settings.	Goldkind (2021)
3.	Develop the rural areas by implementing various technology related to AI and ML.	Mankar et al. (2021)
4.	Organizations should focus on building an environment to adopt AI-enabled tools while also addressing employees' concerns about AI for significant effect of AI.	Jain et al. (2022)

5.3 Implementing AI in Social Development

Social work has long been on the periphery of this ecology that is rapidly changing. The use of "expert systems," neural networks, and other prediction models by social work scholars to improve treatment results was discussed as early as the 1990s. Although the concepts underpinning machine intelligence are not new, the computer power required to make these tools has lately improved to the point that it can now carry out projects that were before unthinkable. We must provide social work faculty and students with a fundamental curriculum on the algorithm, including how it functions, where it is used, how it is deployed, and the opportunities and challenges it presents for integration, if social work is to play a meaningful role in the infusion of AI across all facets of human function [2, 4].

Social work has always been exceptional in meeting human needs. Social workers can envision new AI-enhanced therapeutic tools for individuals, organizations, and communities; mediate between data scientists and organizations in the case of AI; and, most importantly, advocate for justice and equity in the development of policies that shape, manage, and regulate AI [4].

5.4 AI in Social Work

AI solutions are already becoming the standard in social work. At the micro level, artificial intelligence (AI) is being used to reduce the worrisome professional gap between people with mental illness and those who can meet their needs. Recent AI-enhanced treatments in this area include offering customers fast behavioural modification interventions via individualized on-demand virtual counsellors (ODVIC) online. A multimodal embodied conversational agent (ECA), often known as a virtual person who specializes in dialogue-based interactions, is ODVIC, the counsellor. In order to give an evidence-based mental health intervention, the ECA empathically engages with a client, altering verbal and nonverbal communication in real time [2, 5].

AI has great potential for improving customer and employee lives as well as the calibre of services offered by human services organizations. For instance, agencies may utilize predictive analytics, or the use of data to forecast service successes and difficulties, to help with resource allocation decisions. Food banks have teamed with DataKind, a volunteer data science organization, to use historical data and machine learning algorithms to determine a client's level of pantry dependency. By categorizing consumers based on a complex math of need, the organization is able to distribute resources to act to stop a crisis of food insecurity before it escalates. This strategy might be used in various industries and demographics in order to improve the accuracy and efficiency of resource allocation by service organizations [2, 5, 6].

Data collaboratives have been acknowledged at the mezzo level as an innovative way to combine relevant information and data from many industries with real-world difficulties. A key element of data collaboratives is the cooperation of businesses to extract value from data. The effectiveness of these coalitions depends on a data pooling that goes beyond straightforward data interchange. Members and partners search through governmental agencies to create a dynamic online representation of the judicial system [6, 7].

From the use of facial recognition for public safety to the use of chatbots to speed up case management and public access to information in service organizations, AI and its potentials have attracted a lot of interest, excitement, and debate. While the commercial sector employs AI to quickly improve anything from doorbells to personal fitness monitors, cities enthusiastically welcome its application to address challenging social issues. In order to cope with the unavoidable necessity to engage with algorithmic actors like chatbots and other digitally enhanced tools, social work must address the impacts of engaging with embodied algorithms, improve the ability to evaluate data sources, and widen the meaning of collaboration. As we aim for true and informed engagement with augmented and virtual worlds and engage in dialogue with computer agents, such as robots and algorithms, our fundamental concepts of "person" and "environment" may need to be broadened [6].

As in every other business, artificial intelligence is crucial to the social sector. It has already had a big influence on our lives. These numerous examples of how artificial intelligence is changing our way of life—from getting driving instructions on our smartphones to getting daily reminders to exercise more—illustrate how this technology is reshaping our day-to-day activities. With AI's assistance, the UN's Sustainable Development Goals may be in some manner met, which will serve a sizable population in both developed and developing countries. It has already been applied in a number of real-world situations [7, 8].

5.5 Areas of AI for Social Development

AI has several applications for the social advancement of the Indian populace. Healthcare, education, agricultural production, fighting climate change, fostering social inclusion, crisis response, encouraging social entrepreneurship, and many more sectors are primarily covered. The NITI Aayog has launched a significant effort that centres on AI. The initiative focuses primarily on three areas of public life: agriculture, healthcare, and language projects [9].

5.5.1 Healthcare

AI is being used in the healthcare sector. There is potential for artificial intelligence to enhance early illness diagnosis. AI is used to build sophisticated robots that can find and identify malignant cells. By analyzing data from the heart rate sensor, wearables with AI-powered software may identify people at risk for diabetes with up to 85% accuracy. It mixes historical data with medical intelligence in order to develop new drugs [9–13].

5.5.2 Education

AI may be used in educational institutions. It might potentially improve student and instructor production. Adaptive teaching technology can offer topics and courses to students based on their engagement and success with earlier courses and material. With the help of AI, students will be better able to access classes around-the-clock and be guided toward their objectives [9–11].

5.5.3 Agricultural Productivity

Real-time analysis of a variety of factors, including temperature, weather, soil conditions, and water use, can help farmers. Crops can be picked by AI robots more rapidly and in larger numbers than by humans. AI may be used to enhance planning and provide a more plentiful output by determining the best crop selections and the most efficient method to use resources. Small farms have successfully used low-attitude sensors from devices like drones and smartphones to identify crop damage in order to enhance agricultural yield. Additionally, AI can locate weed growth [9, 11, 14].

5.5.4 Environmental Protection

AI innovations can protect the environment from pollution, resource depletion, climate change, and other threats. For instance, the Bay Area non-profit Rainforest Connection employs TensorFlow and other artificial intelligence (AI) techniques to save the world's delicate rainforest ecosystems. In open regions, we can successfully detect and stop illegal logging activities by analyzing the audio-sensor data [9, 15].

5.5.5 Authenticated Information

Due to the increasing accessibility of social media platforms, false and harmful material is purposefully spread to interfere with locals' everyday lives. Our attention must be directed toward stopping or getting rid of inaccurate and misleading information. AI would undoubtedly make it simpler for the general population to access, get, and use reliable, crucial information [16].

5.5.6 Crisis Intervention

There are a number of difficulties that are unique to crises, such as forecasting the development of wildfires and optimizing control tactics for both natural and man-made calamities, in addition to responding to rescue operations and disease outbreaks. By utilizing algorithms and other data that it learns, artificial intelligence may find important information in social media postings. In order to prevent mistakes and ensure that only the most vital information is located and transferred, scientists are concentrating their efforts on improving how the millions of communications are sorted by algorithms [16, 17].

5.6 Prospects and Challenges of AI

There are several aspects proving that artificial intelligence would be prospective for the development of the society, as follows [18–21]:

- Digital assistants will be utilized by a number of highly developed companies to communicate with clients, eliminating the requirement for human employees.
- When combined with other advancements, organizations can employ AI to make robots make choices and take actions more quickly than a human could.
- AI is at the heart of many innovations in practically every field that will assist people in solving most of their complex problems.
- No specific agreement on trade and development to collaborate in order to take advantage of the potential of cutting-edge technologies like blockchain and AI to enhance and grow commerce.
- Companies like Google, Microsoft, and Amazon are also working to meet the government's cloud computing and machine learning requirements. As the Indian government pushes for digital transformation and introduces more AI projects, private enterprises will race to secure significant contracts, contribute to the flow of funding for the development of novel technologies, and launch new AI and data science startups.

5.7 Findings

While there are several prospects of artificial intelligence, India faces several major AI-related challenges that include the following [22–25]:

- The lack of experts in the field of machine learning and also the poor quality of research output being generated.
- In India, there is a dearth of local knowledge on the most recent information being created every day.
- In light of the possibilities, the presently existing Indian businesses and those that are emerging have been reluctant to employ AI.
- India does not have the skilled personnel to apply machine learning to its specific issues and data, despite the availability of many standard programmes.
- Current AI problem-solving techniques are not particularly successful; they must develop in order to handle the complexity of Indian life.

India's digital footprint has expanded significantly overall. The administration is also advancing numerous initiatives in the direction of the goal of technical infrastructure. Different organizations, institutes for artificial intelligence, and industries are creating programmes and policy frameworks to inculcate these skills. The Indian artificial intelligence market, which is still viewed as being in its early stages, can undoubtedly grow significantly with a bit more drive toward the resources and frameworks that would help it expand [26, 27].

Weaker and underrepresented groups of people are at risk because they are typically excluded from discussions regarding AI adoption and its usage as a social engineering tool. In order to offer our ethical viewpoint to the development of algorithmic tools and products, social work has a responsibility to engage in the discussion about a world enriched by AI. Students studying social work require real-world examples, experience, and practice to build the abilities essential to communicate with computer engineers, data scientists, and other disciplines grappling with the advantages and challenges of AI [28, 29].

5.8 Conclusion

The moment has come for individuals and their governments to embrace technology rather than resist change in light of the exponential growth of AI technology. It is also obvious that the complexity of the difficulties brought on by technology is a problem. Given that technology has a worldwide influence, governments and other decision-makers should work with academics to attempt to direct the technology toward benefitting mankind. Researchers and the community should concentrate on bridging the gap between technology and people rather than widening it as computing power increases and more data is produced. As they work together to take action and address the difficulties that technology provides, many organizations, groups, and people are setting global precedents. There are organizations that expose algorithmic unfairness and encourage the individuals to voice their worries and experiences in order to promote best practices and accountability. Global involvement will be aided by the petition to the UN calling for quick action on armed AI. Globally, participation is required for AI to encourage and compel leaders and policy-makers to take the proper steps [28–30].

AI platforms can provide social work students with easier access to opportunities to practise. It would be impractical to involve students in experiential learning because core undergraduate courses are typically taught in lecture halls with a high number of students. Similar to this, although online learning environments have made social work study more accessible to people who otherwise would not be able to do so, online students frequently miss opportunities to connect theory to practice (Washburn & Zhou, 2018). Additionally, institutions must implement cutting-edge, experiential pedagogies, like simulation, to better prepare students to practise before their initial interaction with real customers. Virtual simulation can bridge the gap between the coursework and practicum preparation of the students, even though it is primarily employed in course-level learning [30].

Social work educators need to develop the skill to utilize AI as a pedagogical tool to impart learning among the students to further apply AI techniques for social development. However, the success of this technology's application hinges on how educators use AI to turn it into a useful teaching tool for pupils. This means that instead of using the platform as an individual-level activity right away, the teacher might work with students in a bigger group to engage the platform as a collective learning action to develop a learning community. This would further augment the application of AI by social work practitioners in promoting quality living in the society through social development [2, 6, 28, 30].

References

[1] AI on the Ground: A Snapshot of AI Use in India. (2020 October). *Tandem Research.*

[2] Asakura, K., Occhiuto, K., Todd, S., Leithead, C., & Clapperton, R. (2020). A Call to Action on Artificial Intelligence and Social Work Education: Lessons Learned from A Simulation Project Using Natural Language Processing. *Journal of Teaching in Social Work*, *40*(5), 501–518. https://doi.org/10.1080/08841233.2020.1813234.

[3] Asian Development Bank. (2008). Managing Asian Cities: Sustainable and Inclusive Urban Solutions, *Asian Development Bank Report.* http://www.adb.org/Documents/Studies/Managing-Asian-Cities/mac-report.pdf

[4] Chatterjee, S. (2016). Internet of Things and Social Platforms: An Empirical Analysis from Indian Consumer Behavioral Perspective. *Journal of Behavior & Information Technology*, *39*(2), 133–149. https://doi.org/10. 1080/0144929 X.2019.1587001.

[5] Global Information Society Watch. (2019). Artificial Intelligence: Human Rights, Social Justice and Development. *Association for Progressive Communications* (APC), Article 19, and Swedish International Development Cooperation Agency (SIDA).

[6] Goldkind, L. (2021). Social Work and Artificial Intelligence: Into the Matrix. *Social Service Faculty Publications*. https://doi.org/10.1093/sw/swab028.

[7] Gupta, A. R., & Shahila, Z. (2013). Rural India: The Next Frontier for Social Media Networks. *International Journal of Engineering Research and Technology, 2*(1).

[8] Heeks, R. (2002). Information Systems and Developing Countries: Failure, Success, and Local Improvisations. *The Information Society, 18*(2), 101–112.

[9] NITI Aayog. (2021, February). Responsible AI #AIForAll. https://www.niti.gov.in/sites/default/files/2021-02/Responsible-AI-22022021.pdf.

[10] Hussein, B. R., Halimu, C., & Siddique, M. T. (2020). The Future of Artificial Intelligence and Its Social, Economic and Ethical Consequences, *ICACT*, 17–19.

[11] Jain, R., Garg, N., & Khera, S. N. (2022). Adoption of AI-Enabled Tools in Social Development Organizations in India: An Extension of UTAUT Model. *Frontiers in Psychology, 13*, 893691. https://doi.org/10.3389/fpsyg.2022.893691.

[12] Kejriwal, M. (2019). Crisis Management: Using Artificial Intelligence to Help Save Lives. *Research Outreach.*

[13] Lisetti, C., Amini, R., Yasavur, U., & Rishe, N. (2013). I Can Help You Change! An Empathic Virtual Agent Delivers Behavior Change Health Interventions. *ACM Transactions on Management Information Systems (TMIS), 4*(4), Article 19.

[14] Kolbjørnsrud, V., Amico, R., & Thomas, R.J. (2016). *The Promise of Artificial Intelligence: Redefining Management in the Workforce of the Future.* Accenture. https://www.accenture.com/us-en/insight-promise-artificial-intelligence.

[15] Makridakis, S. (2017). The Forthcoming Artificial Intelligence (AI) Revolution: Its Impact on Society and Firms, *Futures, 90*, 46–60. https://doi.org/10.1016/j.futures.2017.03.006.

[16] Mazumdar, D., & Chattopadhyay, H. K. (2020). Artificial Intelligence and Its Impact on the Society. *International Journal of Law, 6*(5), 306–310.

[17] Mankar, D. V., Jamkar, S. S., & Jakhotiya, P. R. (2021). Artificial Intelligence (AI) in Sustainable Rural Development. *International Engineering Journal for Research & Development, 6*(NCTSRD), 8. https://doi.org/10.17605/OSF.IO/9JSUD.

[18] Nushi, B., Kamar, E., & Horvitz, E. (2018). Towards Accountable AI: Hybrid Human Machine Analyses for Characterizing System Failure. arXiv:1809.07424.

[19] Patterson, D. A., & Cloud, R. N. (1999). The Application of Artificial Neural Networks for Outcome Prediction in a Cohort of Severely Mentally Ill Outpatients. *Journal of Technology for Human Services, 16*(2–3), 47–61.

[20] Punjeta, A. S. (2018). Rural Development with the Help of Artificial Intelligence. *International Journal of Computer Sciences and Engineering, 6*(10), 779–780.

[21] Sachin, S. B., Kadirvel, S., & Ramesh, B. (2020). Significance of Artificial Intelligence in Community Development. *Dogo Ramgsang Research Journal, 10*(6–5), 208–216.

[22] Sarangi, S. S., & Singha, S. (2019). A Survey on Impact of AI and Social Media for Rural Development. *International Journal of Computer Sciences and Engineering, 7*(S11), 64–68.

[23] Bag, S., Srivastava, G., Bashir, M. M. A., Kumari, S., Giannakis, M., & Chowdhury, A. H. (2022). Journey of customers in this digital era: Understanding the role of artificial intelligence technologies in user engagement and conversion. *Benchmarking: An International Journal, 29*(7), 2074–2098.

[24] Thamik, H., & Wu, J. (2022). The Impact of Artificial Intelligence on Sustainable Development in Electronic Markets. *Sustainability, 14*, 3568. https://doi.org/10.3390/su14063568.

[25] Tai, M. C.-t. (2020). The Impact of Artificial Intelligence on Human Society and Bioethics. *Tzu Chi Medical Journal, 32*(4), 339–343. https://doi.org/ 10.4103/tcmj.tcmj_71_20.

[26] Verhulst, S., & Sangokoya, D. (2015, April 22). Data Collaborative: Exchanging Data to Improve People's Lives. https://sverhulst.medium.com/data-collaboratives-exchanging-data-to-improve-people-s-lives-d0fcfc1bdd9a.

[27] Vijay Kumar, S. (2021). Artificial Intelligence – Social Transformation Special Reference to India. *Researchgate*. https://doi.org/ 10.13140/RG.2.2.16751.56483.

[28] Vinuesa, R., Azizpour, H., Leite, I., et al. (2020). The Role of Artificial Intelligence in Achieving the Sustainable Development Goals. *Nature Communications, 11*, 233. https://doi.org/10.1038/s41467-019-14108-y.

[29] Washburn, M., & Zhou, S. (2018). Teaching Note—Technology-Enhanced Clinical Simulations: Tools for Practicing Clinical Skills in Online Social Work Programs. *Journal of Social Work Education, 54*, 554–560. https://doi.org/10.1080/10437797.2017.1404519.

[30] Zhao, J., & Fu, G. (2022). Artificial Intelligence-Based Family Health Education Public Service System. *Frontier in Psychology, 13*, 898107. https://doi.org/10.3389/fpsyg.2022.898107.

Chapter 6

Disease Prediction Using Bayes' Theorem

Swapnali Tandel and Pragya Vaishnav

6.1 Introduction

The development and application of several prominent data mining techniques in a variety of real-world application areas (e.g., industry, healthcare, and bioscience) has resulted in the use of such techniques in machine learning environments, in order to extract useful pieces of information from specified data in healthcare communities, biomedical fields, and so on [1, 2].

Accurate medical database analysis aids early illness prediction, patient treatment, and community services. Machine learning techniques have been effectively applied in a variety of areas, including disease prediction [3]. The goal of constructing a classifier system based on machine learning algorithms is to greatly aid clinicians in predicting and diagnosing illnesses at an early stage [4].

The disease prediction system is based on predictive modelling and forecasts the user's disease based on the symptoms that the user offers as input to the system. The system evaluates the symptoms entered by the user and provides the disease's likelihood as a result [5]. The Naïve Bayes classifier is used for disease prediction [6]. The Naïve Bayes classifier computes the disease's probability. With the rise of big data in the biomedical and healthcare communities, reliable medical data analysis promotes early illness identification and patient treatment [7].

The diagnostic process in clinical practice is based on probabilities and, consequentially, filled with uncertainty [8, 9]. During the process of establishing a diagnosis, the probability of the disease of interest is continuously shifting, either positive or negative, depending on the information gathered during the diagnostic

 DOI: 10.1201/9781003441601-6

process. Important pieces of information for diagnosing a confirmed disease are the results of one or more diagnostic tests. The main goal of diagnostic testing is to Bayes' theorem to rule in or rule out the presence of a disease with a sufficient level of certainty [10]. This paper presents disease prediction using Bayes' theorem.

6.2 Implementation of Naïve Bayes Classifier

6.2.1 Classifier

The applications of classifiers are wide ranging. They find use in medicine, finance, mobile phones, computer vision (face recognition, target tracking), voice recognition, data mining, and uncountable other areas. An example is a classifier that accepts a person's details, such as age, marital status, home address, and medical history, and classifies the person.

6.2.2 Naïve Bayes

In probability theory, Bayes' theorem (often called Bayes' law after Thomas Bayes) relates the conditional and marginal probabilities of two random events. It is often used to compute posterior probabilities given observations [9]. For example, a patient may be observed to have certain symptoms. Bayes' theorem can be used to compute the probability that a proposed diagnosis is correct, given that observation. A naïve Bayes classifier is a term dealing with a simple probabilistic classification based on applying Bayes' theorem.

In simple terms, a naïve Bayes classifier assumes that the presence (or absence) of a particular feature of a class is unrelated to the presence (or absence) of any other feature. For example, a fruit may be considered to be an apple if it is red, round, and about 4 inches in diameter. Even though these features depend on the existence of the other features, a naïve Bayes classifier considers all of these properties to independently contribute to the probability that this fruit is an apple. Depending on the precise nature of the probability model, Naïve Bayes classifiers can be trained very efficiently in supervised learning (Table 6.1).

Table 6.1   Accuracy of the Naïve Bayes Classification

Number of Records in Training Dataset	Number of Records in Testing	Number of Correctly Classified Instances	Number of Incorrectly Classified Instances	Accuracy
303	276	245	31	88.76
303	240	215	25	89.58
303	290	258	32	88.96

6.2.3 Bayesian Theorem

Given training data X, posterior probability of a hypothesis H, P(H|X), follows the Bayes theorem $P(H|X) = P(X|H)P(H)/P(X)$

The Naïve Bayes algorithm is based on Bayesian theorem as given by equation steps in the algorithm as follows:

1. Each data sample is represented by an n dimensional feature vector, $X = (x1, x2 \ldots\ldots xn)$, depicting n measurements made on the sample from n attributes, respectively A1, A2, An.

2. Suppose that there are m classes, C1, C2......Cm. Given an unknown data sample, X (i.e., having no class label), the classifier will predict that X belongs to the class having the highest posterior probability, conditioned if and only if: $P(Ci/X) > P(Cj/X)$ for all $1 <= j <= m$ and $j! = i$. Thus we maximize $P(Ci|X)$. The class Ci for which $P(Ci|X)$ is maximized is called the maximum posteriori hypothesis by Bayes' theorem.

3. Since P(X) is constant for all classes, only $P(X|Ci)P(Ci)$ need be maximized. If the class prior probabilities are not known, then it is commonly assumed that the classes are equally likely, i.e., $P(C1) = P(C2) = \ldots\ldots = P(Cm)$, and we would therefore maximize $P(X|Ci)$. Otherwise, we maximize $P(X|Ci)P(Ci)$. Note that the class prior probabilities may be estimated by $P(Ci) = si/s$, where Si is the number of training samples of class Ci, and s is the total number of training samples on X. That is, the naïve probability assigns an unknown sample X to the class Ci(2).

6.3 Implementation of Bayesian Classification

The Naïve Bayes Classifier technique is mainly applicable when the dimensionality of the inputs is high. Despite its simplicity, Naïve Bayes can often outperform more sophisticated classification methods. The Naïve Bayes model recognizes the characteristics of patients with heart disease. It shows the probability of each input attribute for the predictable state.

6.4 Results and Discussion

The purpose of diagnostic testing is to move from the probability of disease before the diagnostic test (prior probability) to the probability after the diagnostic test based on the test result (posterior probability). A probability principle set forth by mathematician Thomas Bayes (1702–1761), Bayes' theorem is of value in medical decision-making and some of the biomedical sciences (Figure 6.1).

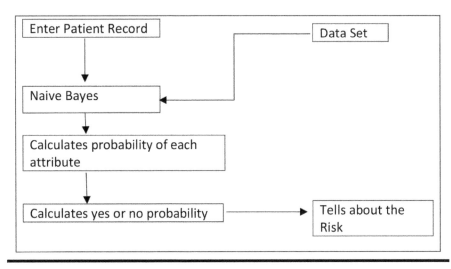

Figure 6.1 Showing predictable state.

An application of Bayes' theorem is in clinical decision-making when it is used to estimate the probability of a particular diagnosis given the appearance of specific signs, symptoms, or test outcomes. Bayes' theorem represents the probabilistic nature of diagnostic reasoning in the form of a mathematical equation. This equation expresses the relationship between probabilities operating during the diagnostic process, showing that the determinants of the posterior probability of disease are the prior probability and the test properties. Bayes' rule is often presented using the language of diagnostic testing, including posterior probabilities (predictive values), sensitivity (Sn) and specificity (Sp), and prior probabilities (often called prevalence; Prev). In many books, equations for Bayes' theorem are typically depicted as follows:

$$PPV = (\text{sensitivity} \times \text{prevalence}) / \left[(\text{sensitivity} \times \text{prevalence}) + ((1 - \text{specificity}) \times (1 - \text{prevalence})) \right]$$

$$NPV = \left[(\text{specificity} \times (\text{prevalence} - 1)) \right] / \left[(1 - \text{sensitivity}) \times (\text{prevalence} + \text{specificity} \times (1 - \text{prevalence})) \right]$$

The antecedent plausibility is called the "prior probability."

The likelihood of the current data given that specific hypothesis is called the "conditional probability."

The rescaled values are called the "posterior probabilities."

The proposed methodology provides treatment, designs, and diagnostics and offers proposals to medicinal services experts that are particular to singular patients (Figures 6.2 to 6.4 and Table 6.2).

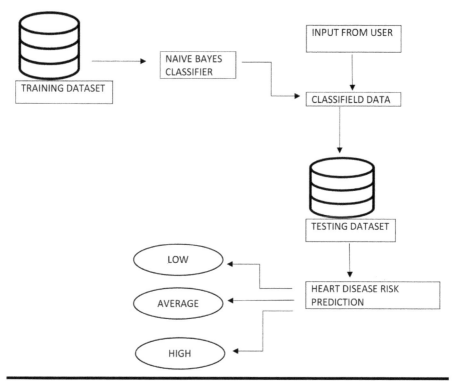

Figure 6.2   Proposed methodology.

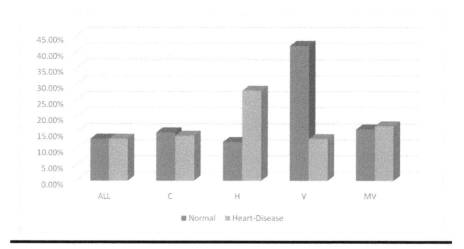

Figure 6.3   Normal versus heart disease.

Table 6.2 Showing Attributes Highlighting Max and Min Values

Age	Sex	Chest Pain Type	Blood Pressure	Cholesterol	Fasting Blood Sugar	Resting ECG	Max Heart Rate	Angina	Peak	Slope	Coloured Vessels	Thai	Class
60	1	4	130	206	0	2	132	1	2.4	2	2	7	0
49	1	2	130	266	0	0	171	0	0.6	1	0	3	1
64	1	1	110	211	0	2	144	1	1.8	2	0	3	1
63	1	4	130	254	0	2	147	0	1.4	2	1	7	0
53	1	4	140	203	1	2	155	0	3.1	3	0	7	0
58	0	1	150	283	1	2	162	1	1	1	0	3	1
58	1	2	120	284	0	2	160	0	1.8	2	0	3	0
58	1	3	132	224	0	2	173	0	3.2	1	2	7	0
63	1	1	145	233	1	2	150	0	2.3	3	0	6	1
67	1	4	160	286	0	2	108	0	1.5	2	3	3	0
67	1	4	120	229	0	2	129	1	2.6	2	2	7	0
37	1	3	130	250	0	0	187	1	3.5	3	0	3	1
41	1	2	130	204	0	2	172	0	1.4	1	0	3	1
56	1	2	120	236	0	0	178	0	0.8	1	0	3	1
62	1	4	140	268	0	2	160	0	3.6	3	2	3	0

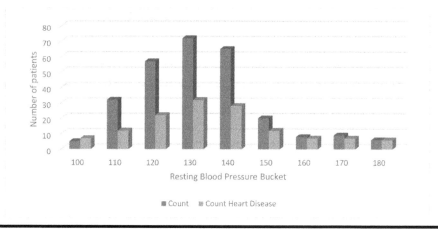

Figure 6.4   Count normal versus count heart disease.

6.5 Data Preparation

In the first stage of the cleaning process, we developed customized procedures to remove noises from the data and prepare it for mining.

In tables, we show the example of the resulting ready-to-mine source data format with 14 attributes. The attribute values of min and max are given in the table.

6.6 Conclusion

Altogether, insight into the use of Bayes' rule in diagnosis is relevant for understanding the interplay between the prior probability of disease and diagnostic test properties in determining the posterior probability of disease.

References

[1] Madni, H. A., Anwar, Z., & Shah, M. A. (2017, September). Data mining techniques and applications—A decade review. In 2017 23rd international conference on automation and computing (ICAC) (pp. 1–7). IEEE.

[2] Birjandi, S. M., & Khasteh, S. H. (2021). A survey on data mining techniques used in medicine. *Journal of Diabetes & Metabolic Disorders, 20*(2), 2055–2071.

[3] Fleuren, L. M., Klausch, T. L., Zwager, C. L., Schoonmade, L. J., Guo, T., Roggeveen, L. F., . . . & Elbers, P. W. (2020). Machine learning for the prediction of sepsis: A systematic review and meta-analysis of diagnostic test accuracy. *Intensive Care Medicine, 46*, 383–400.

[4] Grampurohit, S., & Sagarnal, C. (2020, June). Disease prediction using machine learning algorithms. In *2020 International Conference for Emerging Technology (INCET)* (pp. 1–7). IEEE.

[5] Battineni, G., Sagaro, G. G., Chinatalapudi, N., & Amenta, F. (2020). Applications of machine learning predictive models in the chronic disease diagnosis. *Journal of Personalized Medicine, 10*(2), 21.

[6] Maheswari, S., & Pitchai, R. (2019). Heart disease prediction system using decision tree and naive Bayes algorithm. *Current Medical Imaging, 15*(8), 712–717.

[7] Pingale, K., Surwase, S., Kulkarni, V., Sarage, S., & Karve, A. (2019). Disease prediction using machine learning. *International Research Journal of Engineering and Technology (IRJET), 6*, 831–833.

[8] Bours, M. J. (2021). Bayes' rule in diagnosis. *Journal of Clinical Epidemiology, 131*, 158–160.

[9] Alizadehsani, R., Roshanzamir, M., Hussain, S., Khosravi, A., Koohestani, A., Zangooei, M. H., . . . & Acharya, U. R. (2021). Handling of uncertainty in medical data using machine learning and probability theory techniques: A review of 30 years (1991–2020). *Annals of Operations Research*, 1–42.

[10] McKay, K. M., Lim, L. L., & Van Gelder, R. N. (2021). Rational laboratory testing in uveitis: A Bayesian analysis. *Survey of Ophthalmology, 66*(5), 802–825.

Chapter 7

Secure Voting System Using Blockchain Technology

Shalu J. Rajawat, Manju Kaushik,
and Surendra Kumar Yadav

7.1 Introduction

Building a secure electronic voting system that offers the fairness and privacy of current voting schemes, while providing the transparency and flexibility offered by electronic systems, has been a challenge for a long time [1–3]. In this project, we evaluate an application of blockchain as a service to implement distributed electronic voting systems [4, 5]. The project proposes an electronic voting system based on blockchain that addresses some of the limitations in existing systems and evaluates some of the popular blockchain frameworks for the purpose of constructing a blockchain-based e-voting system [6]. In particular, we evaluate the potential of distributed ledger technologies through the process of an election, and the implementation of a blockchain-based application, which improves the security and decreases the cost of hosting a nationwide election [7]. Moreover, we also evaluate the use of cryptography which is the basic foundation of blockchain. The cryptographic algorithm that is being used in blockchain and cryptocurrencies is the SHA-256. SHA is the abbreviation for Secure Hash Algorithm, and here, 256 stands for the number of bits [8]. Without going into technical of the algorithm, let's just focus on the drawback of it. The most basic question is how secure the SHA-256 is and the answer to this question is that SHA-256 is one of the most secure hashing functions on the market [9]. The US government requires its agencies to protect certain sensitive information

DOI: 10.1201/9781003441601-7

using SHA (www.doncio.navy.mil/chips/ArticleDetails.aspx?ID=7375256). Three properties make SHA-256 this secure. Firstly, it is almost impossible to reconstruct the initial data from the hash value. A brute-force attack would need to make 2,256 attempts to generate the initial data. Secondly, having two messages with the same hash value (called a collision) is extremely unlikely. With 2,256 possible hash values (more than the number of atoms in the known universe), the likelihood of two being the same is infinitesimally, unimaginably small. Finally, a minor change to the original data alters the hash value so much that it's not apparent the new hash value is derived from similar data; this is known as the avalanche effect [10].

7.2 UML and General Architecture

To understand the flow of application first we can understand the Unified Modeling Language (UML) diagram and general architecture of the blockchain working process and application working with blockchain technology. This UML and general architecture define the common flow of any application built with the facility of blockchain technology and its decentralized system. With this architecture and use case, we can easily understand the flow of application.

7.3 Configuration and Working of APP

The following is a detailed description of every component of the application, and its functionality with used tools and technologies (Figure 7.1). There are several components in the application, described in this section.

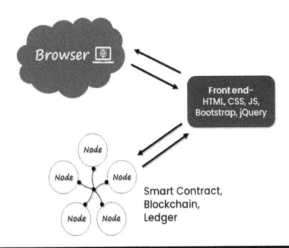

Figure 7.1   General architecture.

7.3.1 MetaMask Configuration

First you have to configure the MetaMask extension in order to manage our blockchain transactions and connect to the Ethereum Node RPC (Ganache in our case). Click on the drop-down list for the list of networks and then select Custom RPC (Figures 7.2 and 7.3).

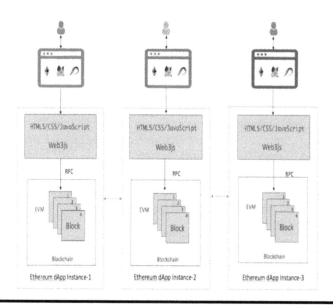

Figure 7.2   UML diagram.

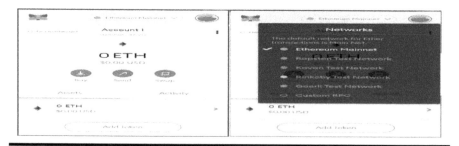

Figure 7.3   MetaMask configuration.

Source: Adapted from https://community.metamask.io/t/how-to-add-custom-networks-to-metamask-like-binance-and-polygon-matic/3634

https://wiki.rugdoc.io/docs/how-to-connect-metamask-to-the-binance-smart-chain-network-bsc/

7.3.2 Ganache

Now we will start our Ganache application and create a new Ethereum localhost Node. It will create 10 nodes. Here we will use the link of RPC Server and Network ID and feed it into our Custom RPC Network of MetaMask. Here our RPC Server link is http://127.0.0.1:7545/ hence it works on port 7545 of the localhost and the network ID by default is 1337 but our Ganache network ID is 5777 (as shown in red block in Figures 7.4 and 7.5 below). The Network ID is also known as Chain ID. Once the MetaMask configuration of Ganache local RPC is done, we are ready to go.

Figure 7.4   Ganache workspace creation.

Source: Adapted from https://trufflesuite.com/docs/ganache/how-to/workspaces/create-workspaces/

Figure 7.5   Ganache setup for application.

Source: Adapted from https://trufflesuite.com/ganache/

7.3.3 Truffle

To start Truffle, visit the file explorer and open your project; now open the command prompt at the root directory of the project and enter the following command: "truffle migrate—reset." This command will start the Truffle framework and will compile and deploy the smart contracts to the blockchain. Here, the reset command is used to overwrite the previously deployed smart contracts (Figures 7.6 to 7.12).

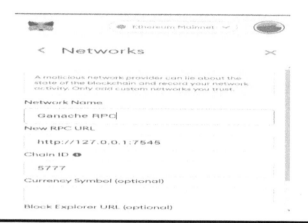

Figure 7.6   Network setup.

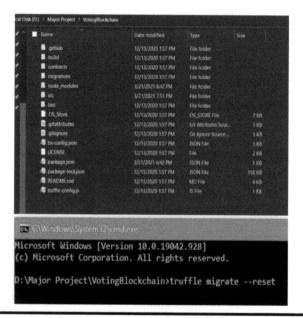

Figure 7.7   Truffle execution.

Figure 7.8   Truffle setup.

Figure 7.9   Truffle setup done.

7.3.4 Testing the Contracts (Using Chai and Mocha)

Now we will test our smart contract using the code we have written using the two testing libraries/framework. To test the contracts, we will use the Truffle command test, i.e., Truffle test, and it will test the smart contracts based upon the test cases we have written in the assertion code.

7.3.5 Starting the Browser-Sync Lite Server

Now we will start our lite server to start our webpage. We have used jQuery and several front-end frameworks to make the webpage dynamic. To start the lite server, we have to type in the command "npm run dev" at the root directory of the project as shown. This will start the server on localhost 3000, i.e., port 3000. To exit the server, you can press ctrl ^C. Here the connection of blockchain with the front-end is done using the Web3.js library which is a JavaScript library to manage our smart contracts and add functionalities of modifying the blockchain to front-end components.

7.3.6 Importing Account to MetaMask from Ganache

Now we will import account into MetaMask through Ganache. To import any account, we just need the private key. The private key should be kept confidential because it is the only key one needs to access your account. Click on account information in Ganache and copy the private key. Now go to MetaMask and click on import account and enter the private key string there as shown. After import it will show the total amount of ETH (99.9713 ETH in our case).

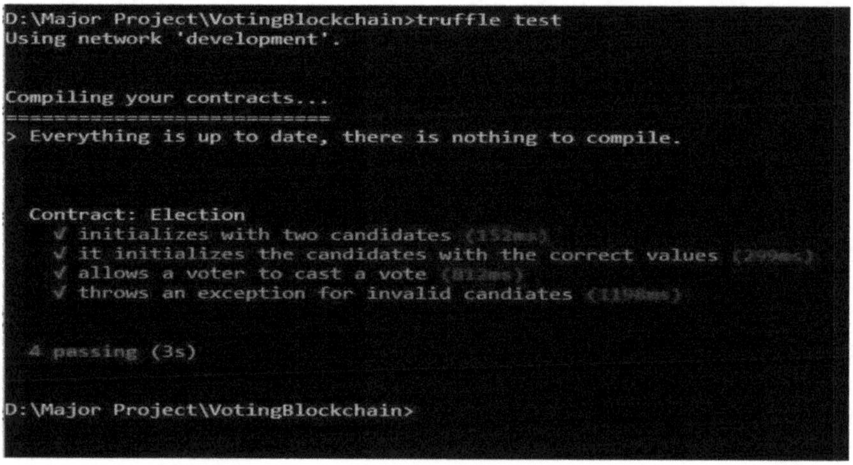

Figure 7.10   Testing contracts.

```
D:\Major Project\VotingBlockchain>npm run dev

> pet-shop@1.0.0 dev D:\Major Project\VotingBlockchain
> lite-server

** browser-sync config **
{
  injectChanges: false,
  files: [ './**/*.{html,htm,css,js}' ],
  watchOptions: { ignored: 'node_modules' },
  server: {
    baseDir: [ './src', './build/contracts' ],
    middleware: [ [Function], [Function] ]
  }
}
[Browsersync] Access URLs:
 --------------------------------------
       Local: http://localhost:3000
    External: http://192.168.106.1:3000
 --------------------------------------
          UI: http://localhost:3001
 UI External: http://localhost:3001
 --------------------------------------
[Browsersync] Serving files from: ./src
[Browsersync] Serving files from: ./build/contracts
[Browsersync] Watching files...
21.05.12 12:21:39 200 GET /index.html
21.05.12 12:21:39 200 GET /css/styles.css
21.05.12 12:21:39 200 GET /css/bootstrap.min.css
21.05.12 12:21:39 200 GET /js/bootstrap.min.js
21.05.12 12:21:39 200 GET /js/app.js
21.05.12 12:21:39 200 GET /images/voteLogo.jpg
21.05.12 12:21:39 200 GET /js/web3.min.js
```

Figure 7.11   Browser-sync lite server.

Figure 7.12   Import account from MetaMask to Ganache.

Source: Adapted from www.geeksforgeeks.org/how-to-set-up-ganche-with-metamask/

7.3.7 Voting through the Front-End Webpage

Now we will open our webpage and here, we can see that each candidate has a vote count of 0. Also, our account is connected to the front-end using MetaMask (the same account that we imported from Ganache) (Figures 7.13 and 7.19).

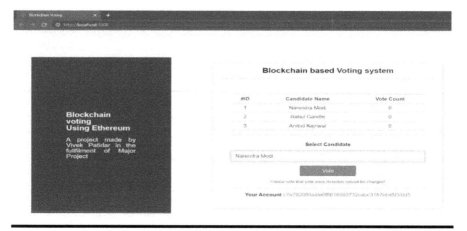

Figure 7.13 Front-end page.

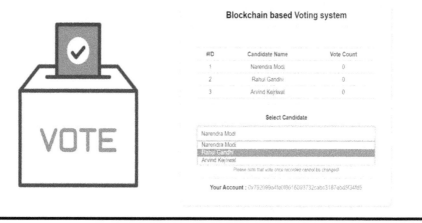

Figure 7.14 Select candidate page.

Now we will select the candidate we want to vote for from the dropdown list.

After selecting the candidate, we will click on vote and it will initiate a transaction on blockchain. We have to confirm the transaction through MetaMask as shown and then our vote will be cast successfully. One account can vote only once.

Now if we import another account from Ganache into our MetaMask, the webpage will be reloaded with the new account and now you can vote with the new account as shown.

You can note here that the account address has changed from that of the previous account. Now on clicking vote and confirming the transaction, our vote will be cast as shown.

Figure 7.15   One account votes once.

Figure 7.16   Confirm transaction with MetaMask.

Since with one account we have voted for candidate 1 and with another account we have voted for candidate 2, we can see the total number of votes for each candidate as shown.

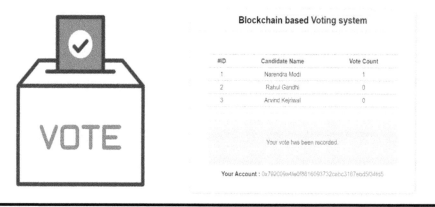

Figure 7.17   Approval page.

Figure 7.18   For new account vote.

Figure 7.19   Account detail changed.

7.3.8 Reviewing the Transactions That Happened in Ganache

Now we can open the blockchain in Ganache and see all the transactions that took place in our blockchain. Click on an individual transaction to view its details (such as Sender Address, To Contract Address, Value, Gas Used, Gas Price, Gas Limit, Mined in Block, and Transaction Data) as shown in the figures. Here, Gas is the fee, or pricing value, required to successfully conduct a transaction or execute a contract on the Ethereum blockchain. Also, you can view your entire blockchain along with blocks and their details as shown (Figures 7.20 to 7.23).

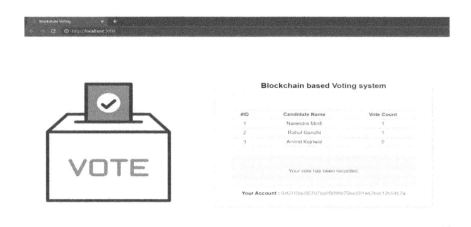

Figure 7.20   Total number of voters.

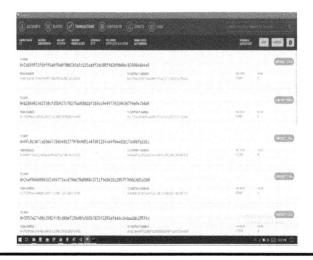

Figure 7.21   Blockchain along with blocks.

Figure 7.22   Each block.

Figure 7.23   Details of individual sender.

7.4 Conclusion

Making the election process cheap and quick normalizes it in the eyes of the voters, removes a certain power barrier between the voter and the elected official, and puts a certain amount of pressure on the elected official. It also opens the door for a more direct form of democracy in countries such as India, allowing voters to express their will on individual bills and propositions. In this decentralized application, this chapter introduced a unique, blockchain-based electronic voting system that utilizes smart contracts to enable secure and cost-efficient election while guaranteeing voter privacy. This chapter outlined the system's architecture, the design, and a security analysis of the system that show how the blockchain technology offers a new possibility for democratic countries to advance from the pen-and-paper election scheme to a more cost- and time-efficient election scheme, while increasing the security. This application consists of adding the functionalities to the admin panel to add political leaders after the deployment of the smart contract. Once the smart contracts are deployed, the leader's name should be synchronized at the run time using the admin address. This application can be used to conduct elections where one can create election using the respective political parties and leaders. Once created, the application should be hosted and available to every citizen. Every citizen would have a private key and a public key and it consists of the fingerprint and Aadhaar card authentication. The voter's ID would be anonymous since his/her private address would not be known by anyone, but he can use his public ID to vote for the candidate. This application could be used by just paying the ETH Gas during the transaction and the vote will be cast. It can be a replacement of the normal pen-paper voting, or the EVM voting, that consists of some security concerns such as modification of machines, ballot hijack, domination by political leaders, corruption, etc.

7.5 Future Scope

A limitation of this system is that it does not implement an OTP (one-time password) option in the registration process. Another limitation is that we stored encrypted votes on the blockchain during voting. After the election is over, this data will no longer be used. The cost of storing this data has increased. The aforementioned limitations will be part of future work. Therefore, by using dual currencies, we aim to use sidechains in the proposed way. Therefore, we can store the encrypted audio on the sidechain and use the decrypted result on the mainchain to reduce costs.

References

[1] Jafar, U., Aziz, M. J. A., & Shukur, Z. (2021). Blockchain for electronic voting system—review and open research challenges. Sensors, 21(17), 5874.

[2] Huang, J., He, D., Obaidat, M. S., Vijayakumar, P., Luo, M., & Choo, K. K. R. (2021). The application of the blockchain technology in voting systems: A review. ACM Computing Surveys (CSUR), 54(3), 1–28.

[3] Al-Maaitah, S., Qatawneh, M., & Quzmar, A. (2021, July). E-voting system based on blockchain technology: A survey. In 2021 International Conference on Information Technology (ICIT) (pp. 200–205). IEEE.

[4] Pawlak, M., & Poniszewska-Marańda, A. (2021). Trends in blockchain-based electronic voting systems. Information Processing & Management, 58(4), 102595.

[5] Alvi, S. T., Uddin, M. N., Islam, L., & Ahamed, S. (2022). DVTChain: A blockchain-based decentralized mechanism to ensure the security of digital voting system voting system. Journal of King Saud University-Computer and Information Sciences, 34(9), 6855–6871.

[6] Li, C., Xiao, J., Dai, X., & Jin, H. (2021). AMVchain: Authority management mechanism on blockchain-based voting systems. Peer-to-Peer Networking and Applications, 14(5), 2801–2812.

[7] Abuidris, Y., Kumar, R., Yang, T., & Onginjo, J. (2021). Secure large-scale E-voting system based on blockchain contract using a hybrid consensus model combined with sharding. Etri Journal, 43(2), 357–370.

[8] Taş, R., & Tanrıöver, Ö. Ö. (2021). A manipulation prevention model for blockchain-based e-voting systems. *Security and Communication Networks, 2021*, 1–16.

[9] Anwar ul Hassan, C., Hammad, M., Iqbal, J., Hussain, S., Ullah, S. S., AlSalman, H., . . . & Arif, M. (2022). A liquid democracy enabled blockchain-based electronic voting system. *Scientific Programming, 2022*, 1–10.

[10] Malkawi, M., Yassein, M. B., & Bataineh, A. (2021). Blockchain based voting system for Jordan parliament elections. International Journal of Electrical and Computer Engineering, 11(5), 4325.

Chapter 8

Malware Analysis
An Experimental Approach

Nikita Patil, Amit Kumar Singh, and Sushil Kumar

8.1 Introduction

Malicious software, known as malware, is designed with harmful intent to help attackers achieve their objectives. It includes software intentionally created to carry out harmful actions and disrupt computer systems, gather personal information without consent, and pose a threat to the Internet's availability, host integrity, and user security [1].

Malware comes in various forms, such as viruses, worms, Trojan horses, rootkits, backdoors, botnets, spyware, and adware, and these categories are not entirely distinct, often exhibiting characteristics of multiple classes simultaneously. Malware is a significant and persistent security threat to the Internet, as evidenced by surveys indicating a rising number of malware-related incidents and network breaches in recent years [2]. The volume, sophistication, and speed of malware continue to grow [3].

Today's malware is more sophisticated and employs new techniques to target computers and mobile devices. With over 100,000 new malware samples being identified daily, cyber threats have become more targeted, persistent, and covert [4]. Modern malware uses various techniques, such as hiding, replicating, and bypassing host protections, making it challenging for traditional defenses like firewalls and antivirus software, which rely on signature-based detection [5].

To address the limitations of signature-based approaches, malware analysis techniques have been developed, including static and dynamic analysis. These methods assist analysts in understanding the threats and intentions behind malicious code

DOI: 10.1201/9781003441601-8

samples. The insights gained from malware analysis can help respond to emerging malware trends and take preventive measures against future threats [6]. By studying malware elements, analysts can identify and classify unknown malware into existing families. This research paper provides a comprehensive survey of methods and approaches used for analyzing and classifying malware executables [7].

8.2 Malware Basics

As PC code intended to meddle with a PC's conventional working, malware is a sweeping term for infections, Trojans, and distinctive harming PC programs threat actors use to taint frameworks and organizations in order to accomplish admittance to delicate information [8].

Malware (short for malicious software) could be a document or code, typically conveyed over an organization, that contaminates, investigates, takes, or directs almost any conduct an aggressor wants. What's more, since malware comes in such a great deal of variations, there are shifted techniques to taint PC frameworks [9].

The following are the types of malware (Figure 8.1):

■ Adware: Adware is a form of malware that automatically displays ads and promotions on your device. It is the most profitable type of malware but is considered the least dangerous.

■ Spyware: Spyware is designed to monitor and track web activities and other user actions. Similar to adware, it often sends data to advertisers. Spyware can invade privacy and may be exploited for malicious purposes, raising concerns about its use [10].

■ Virus: A virus is a malicious computer code created by cyber criminals to replicate itself. Infections can be utilized to make botnets, take information, coerce cash, and harm PCs, from there; the sky is the limit. They normally spread through document division among PCs or tainted programming bundles [10].

■ Worm: A worm is a type of virus that self-replicates and spreads rapidly. It can destroy files and information on a computer. Worms propagate across computer networks by exploiting software vulnerabilities. Various types of malicious programs fall under the category of computer worms, and they are often spread through mass emails with infected links to users' contacts [11].

■ Trojan: It deceives users by masquerading as legitimate software. It is one of the most dangerous types of malware. Trojans are used to steal financial data, gather information (logins, financial details), modify files, seize control of a computer's system resources, and more [12].

■ Backdoor: A secondary passage gives unapproved admittance to a PC organization, permitting other malware to enter, or empowering programmers to send spam or execute assaults.

Figure 8.1   Malware categories.

Source: Adapted from https://infosecwriteups.com/malware-analysis-101-ac6d55092c8d

- Keyloggers: Keyloggers record all keystrokes made on a computer without the user's consent to acquire login passwords, usernames, and other sensitive information.
- Ransomware: Ransomware is malicious software that encrypts all files on a computer and leaves messages demanding a ransom for data recovery. It typically spreads like a traditional computer worm through network vulnerabilities or downloaded files. The data is encrypted using a key known only to the attackers [13].

8.3 Malware Analysis

Malware analysis involves the study of how the malware operates and the potential consequences of a particular malware strain. Malicious code can vary significantly, and it's crucial to recognize that malware can possess multiple functionalities, taking the form of viruses, worms, spyware, and Trojan horses. Each type of malware clandestinely collects data from the infected device without the user's knowledge or consent [14].

The purpose of malware analysis is to acquire essential information to combat malware attacks. This includes understanding the system's behavior, locating the infected file, uncovering the mechanisms employed by the malware, and identifying the specific category of malware to which it belongs. Malware comes in various forms, and conducting effective malware analysis requires precise techniques and methodologies to achieve the study's objectives [15].

8.4 Methods of Malware Analysis

During malware analysis, the malware sample typically comes in a. exe file format, which is not easily readable by humans. Subsequently, explicit procedures are utilized to separate data from the malware. There are two principal ways to deal with malware investigation: static examination and dynamic investigation. Each of these strategies can further be categorized as either basic or advanced [16] (Figures 8.2 to 8.7).

Basic Static Analysis: Malicious projects are scanned using antivirus tools, then hashed and detected when packed or obfuscated within the program. To identify the packer program used and extract the malware file, PEiD is employed. The compact executable format of the program is examined [17].

High-Level Static Examination: The high-level static examination stage includes dismantling or troubleshooting to research strings, libraries, and capabilities utilizing the IDA disassembler.

Essential Unique Examination: The fundamental strategy in powerful examination involves noticing the way of behaving of malware in a virtual machine to try not to think twice about the principal framework if the executed malware ends up being destructive.

High-Level Unique Examination: In cutting-edge dynamic investigation strategies, the Windows operating system is dissected, and library examination and checking methods are utilized, alongside information investigation bundles made by malware.

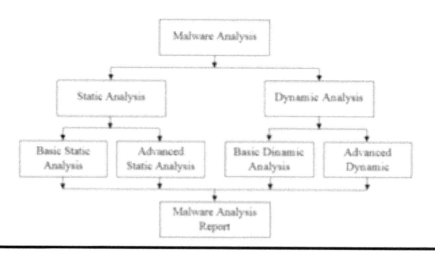

Figure 8.2   Categories of malware analysis.

Source: Adapted from https://iopscience.iop.org/article/10.1088/1742-6596/1140/1/012042/pdf

Malware Examination Report: Reports of malware investigation results are acquired from both static and dynamic examinations. These reports give data in regard to the attributes of the malware [18].

This document presents the results of analyzing a malware sample, focusing on various high- and low-level elements. The report covers aspects such as the main purpose of the sample, its modification of auto-execute functionality through registry settings/creation, writing data to a remote process, and the sample's evasion strategies to remain undetected and avoid suspicion [19].

8.5 General Information

The analysis in this document is based on the following sample. The file name is ab65eebe0f96d3787893329992670ff97621c76e2d8c1be366c00429c944350b

FILE SIZE: 1.23MB (1291264 bytes)
MD5: 8EABDFF3D7D6BD826C109A37B10B218B
SHA-1: 3CCB0C1CE3E8F3DF3732DB47B15DE253A0C08215

An examination of the static properties of the file reveals that the file is a 32-bit Dynamic Link Library for the Microsoft Windows operating system.

ab65eebe0f96d3787893329992670

Property	Value
File Name	C:\Users\nikita\Downloads\sample\ab65eebe0f96d3787893329992670...
File Type	Portable Executable 32
File Info	UPX v3.0
File Size	1.23 MB (1291264 bytes)
PE Size	58.00 KB (59392 bytes)
Created	Wednesday 28 April 2021, 13.35.42
Modified	Thursday 08 July 2021, 11.35.14
Accessed	Thursday 08 July 2021, 11.35.46
MD5	8EABDFF3D7D6BD826C109A37B10B218B
SHA-1	3CCB0C1CE3E8F3DF3732DB47B15DE253A0C08215

Property	Value
CompanyName	Microsoft Corporation.
FileDescription	BitLocker 驱动器加密服务实用工具
FileVersion	6.1.7600.16385
InternalName	BitLocker.exe
LegalCopyright	© Microsoft Corporation. All rights reserved.
OriginalFilename	BitLocker.exe
ProductName	Microsoft® Windows® Operating System

Figure 8.3 **Showing static properties of file.**

8.6 Detecting Packers and Protectors

Malware samples are often protected by so called packers and protectors. Packers and protectors are dedicated tools intended to obfuscate and rewrite executable file structure in order to evade detection by antivirus (AV) products and hinder further analysis. There are two popular tools to detect packers' signatures: PEiD and Exeinfo PE. Using both the tools confirms that the sample is most likely packed by UPX.

To unpack the sample I used the online unpacker tool which extracted two .bin files.

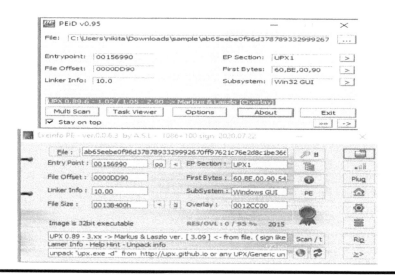

Figure 8.4   Exeinfo PE window—UPX packer detected.

Source: Adapted from https://tech-zealots.com/reverse-engineering/dissecting-manual-unpacking-of-a-upx-packed-file/

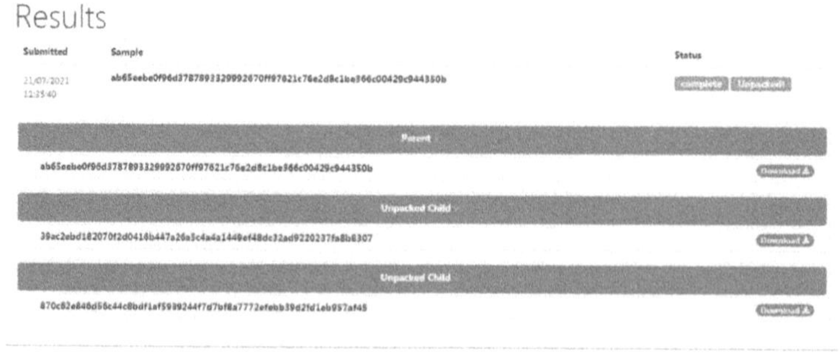

Figure 8.5   Unpacked sample.

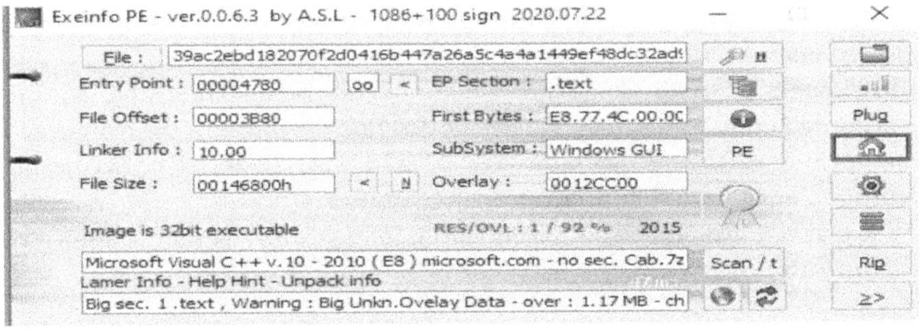

Figure 8.6 Checking unpacked sample1 in Exeinfo PE.

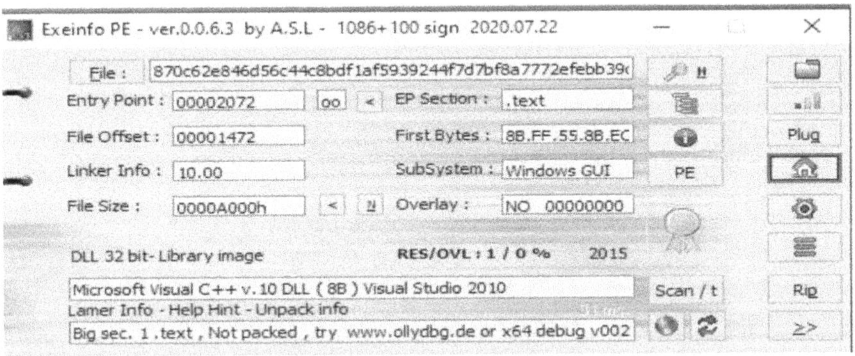

Figure 8.7 Checking unpacked sample2 in Exeinfo PE.

Source: Adapted from https://stackoverflow.com/questions/55892539/how-to-detect-if-malware-is-packed-or-not

To verify if it was successfully unpacked and is not protected by any other protector, open both. bin files in Exeinfo PE.

Based on new Exeinfo PE results we can assume that the malware sample is not protected by another packer and was likely compiled using Microsoft Visual C++ v.10.

8.7 Analyzing Malware Sample on VirusTotal

VirusTotal is used to analyze suspicious files and URLs to detect types of malware and automatically share them with the security community.

After submitting the file in the website we see the detailed analysis of the unpacked malware file.

In Figure 8.8, we see some vendors that can detect the malware, but don't list the malware family name. Their detections describe the threat in the most generic terms, including "Unsafe", "Win/malicious_confidence_100% (W)", "Malicious", "Heuristic", or "Trojan.Autoruns.GenericKD.42681374".

The malware was created on 18 April 2015. In Figure 8.9, we see the history and file information.

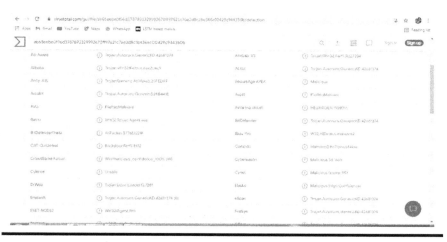

Figure 8.8   Malware list of some vendors.

Figure 8.9   History and file information.

An X.509 certificate is a digital certificate based on the widely accepted International Telecommunications Union (ITU) X.509 standard, which defines the format of public key infrastructure (PKI) certificates. They are used to manage identity and security in Internet communications and computer networking. They are unobtrusive and ubiquitous, and we encounter them every day when using websites, mobile apps, online documents, and connected devices.

Here we see that the aop_unpacked.exe sample is importing functions from many different libraries. We then analyze what functions are imported from each library, and search for functions that might point to some of the malware functionalities. The following is a list of a few more interesting functions.

CreateRemoteThread and *WriteProcessMemory* functions present in kernel32.dll library are indicators that malware is injecting threads into other system processes. Most likely the intention is to hide its presence in the system or to tamper and interact with other processes (e.g., *information stealing*). *TerminateProcess* function suggests that malware might be trying to terminate some system processes. Knowing from the strings analysis that the malware has hardcoded names of antivirus programs processes, we may guess that it will be trying to kill those processes to avoid detection.

The *WinExec* function suggests the malware might be trying to execute some system command. Since avicap32.dll is used for registry operations, the malware is probably performing some registry operations. Also, the presence of the function *CreateServiceA* suggests that the malware might create a system service probably as a persistence mechanism (Figure 8.10).

The system clipboard functions of user32.dll suggest that the malware might be trying to monitor the system clipboard. It is another indicator of information stealing malware functionality. *InternetOpenUrlA* function from wininet.dll is used to retrieve data from an FTP or HTTP location. Malware might be using this function to download additional configuration information from the Internet.

Analyzing both VirusTotal and sandbox results:

■ Modifies auto-execute functionality by setting/creating a value in the registry
■ Writes data to a remote process
■ Two malicious files were extracted named RAVCplscv.exe and RAVCplscv.exe.bin labeled "Trojan.Autoruns.GenericKD"
■ Reads the active computer name

"<Input Sample.exe"

(Path:"HKLM\SYSTEM\CONTROLSET001\CONTROL\COMPUTER NAME\ACTIVECOMPUTERNAME"; Key: "COMPUTERNAME")

"RAVCplscv.exe"

(Path:"HKLM\SYSTEM\CONTROLSET001\CONTROL\COMPUTER NAME\ACTIVECOMPUTERNAME"; Key: "COMPUTERNAME") "cscript.exe"

(Path:"HKLM\SYSTEM\CONTROLSET001\CONTROL\COMPUTER NAME\ACTIVECOMPUTERNAME";Key:"COMPUTERNAME")

- Reads the cryptographic machine GUID
- Possibly tries to evade analysis by sleeping many times "RAVCplscv.exe" (Thread ID: 2936) slept "520" times (threshold: 500)
- Opens the MountPointManager (often used to detect additional infection locations)
- Writes data to a remote process

"<Input Sample.exe" wrote 32 bytes to a remote process "%WINDIR%\System32\cscript.exe" (Handle: 244)

"<Input Sample.exe" wrote 52 bytes to a remote process "%WINDIR%\System32\cscript.exe" (Handle: 244)

"<Input Sample.exe" wrote 4 bytes to a remote process "%WINDIR%\System32\cscript.exe" (Handle: 244)

"<Input Sample.exe" wrote 32 bytes to a remote process "%COMMONPROGRAMFILES%\microsoft shared\Triedit\RAVC plscv.exe" (Handle: 28) "<Input Sample.exe" wrote 52 bytes to a remote process "%COMMONPROGRAMFILES%\microsoft shared\ Triedit\RAVCplscv.exe" (Handle: 28) "<Input Sample.exe" wrote 4 bytes to a remote process "%COMMONPROGRAMFILES%\ microsoft shared\Triedit\RAVCplscv.exe" (Handle: 28)

- The YARA signature matched
- Contacted hosts and countries

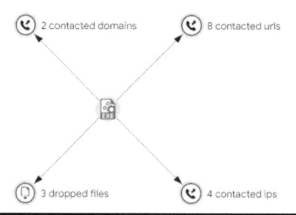

Figure 8.10

Conclusion

The process of identifying and analyzing suspicious files on endpoints and within networks via dynamic analysis, static analysis, or complete reverse engineering is known as malware analysis. In this paper, a method of malware analysis is described, together with a report of its application. The analysis technique described in this work is methodical and rigorous, with information acquisition and a thorough comprehension of a specific malware as its primary goals.

References

[1] Bayer, U., Moser, A., Kruegel, C., & Kirda, E. (2006). Dynamic analysis of malicious code. *Journal in Computer Virology, 2*, 67–77.

[2] *The need for speed: 2013 incident response survey.* (2013). Retrieved January 10, 2023, from www.inforisktoday.in/surveys/2013-incident-response-survey-s-18

[3] Micro, T. (2012). *Addressing big data security challenges: The right tools for smart protection.* Trend Micro.

[4] Gandotra, E., Bansal, D., & Sofat, S. (2014). Malware analysis and classification: A survey. *Journal of Information Security, 5*(12), 56–64.

[5] Next Generation Threats. (2013). Retrieved November 12, 2022, from www.fireeye.com/threat-protection/

[6] You, I., & Yim, K. (2010, November). Malware obfuscation techniques: A brief survey. In *2010 International conference on broadband, wireless computing, communication and applications* (pp. 297–300). IEEE.

[7] Megira, S., Pangesti, A. R., & Wibowo, F. W. (2018, December). Malware analysis and detection using reverse engineering technique. *Journal of Physics: Conference Series, 1140*(1), 012042.

[8] Utama, H., & Wibowo, F. W. (2015, December). Security specification of WS-SecureConversation. In *2015 IEEE student conference on research and development (SCOReD)* (pp. 690–695). IEEE.

[9] Prayudi, Y., & Riadi, I. (2015). Implementation of malware analysis using static and dynamic analysis method. *International Journal of Computer Applications, 117*(6).

[10] Nugroho, H. A., & Hamid. (2013). Reverse engineering techniques for malware analysis. In *International symposium on digital forensics and security* (ISDFS'13), Elazığ, Turkey, 20–21 May 2013, pp. 172–176.

[11] Uppal, D., Mehra, V., & Verma, V. (2014). Basic survey on malware analysis, tools and techniques. *International Journal on Computational Sciences & Applications (IJCSA), 4*(1), 103.

[12] Baskaran, B., & Ralescu, A. (2016). A study of android malware detection techniques and machine learning. In *Proceedings of MAICS 2016*, pp. 15–23.

[13] Hutauruk, S. C. Y., Yulianto, F. A., & Satrya, G. B. (2016). Malware analysis pada windows operating system Untuk Mendeteksi Trojan. *e-Proceding of Enggineering, 3*(2), 3590–3595.

[14] Agrawal, M., Singh, H., Gour, N., & Kumar, M. A. (2014). Evaluation on malware analysis. *International Journal of Computer Science and Information Technologies, 5*(3), 3381–3383.

[15] Alfalqi, K., Alghamdi, R., & Waqdan, M. (2015). Android platform malware analysis. *International Journal of Advanced Computer Science and Applications (IJACSA)*, 6(1), 140–146.

[16] Zeltser, L. (2001). *Reverse engineering malware*. https://zeltser.com/reverse-engineering-malware-methodology/.

[17] Almarri, S., & Sant, P. (2014). Optimised malware detection in digital forensics. *International Journal of Network Security & Its Applications*, 6(1), 1.

[18] Wibowo, F. W. (2012). Interoperability of reconfiguring system on FPGA using a design entry of hardware description *ACEEE International Journal on Information Technology*, 2(01), 60–64.

[19] Sikorski, M., & Honig, A. (2012). *Practical malware analysis: The hands-on guide to dissecting malicious software*. No Starch Press.

Chapter 9

Deployment of New Life Cycle Model for Applications of Web

Deepika Shekhawat and Anuj Kalwar

9.1 Introduction

The paradigm of development has shifted from desktop rich applications to web-based applications. This has made the Internet a plethora of multi-domain web applications that harness the power of Internet-based technologies for accomplishing various objectives such as legacy systems, information systems, databases, work-flow management, distributed knowledge, cooperative work, media sharing and many others. Web applications have now become a dominant and highly attractive platform for deploying business and are extensively used in information delivery platforms, social networking sites, e-learning environments, ecommerce systems and many others.

A web application can be defined as a program that makes use of web-based technologies and can be accessed by a web browser (Okanovic, 2014). The break-through in web application development technologies inexorably represents a quantum leap in the advancement and penetration of the World Wide Web, or simply the web. The Internet has pervaded every aspect of our existence and has redefined our choices of life and work (Figure 9.1).

Most of the web applications are not carefully planned and face security breaches, site crash, server overload and performance failures. This scenario leads to loss of customers and consequently loss in revenue, devaluation of stocks and blemished reputation. In a more aggravated situation, the company may face permanent

DOI: 10.1201/9781003441601-9

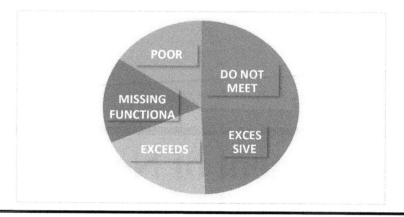

Figure 9.1   Challenges faced in web application development.

Source: Cutter Research Briefs, 2000

loss of customers as well as lawsuits (Williams, 2001). The legal implications levied on a company if the web application fails can be found in (Verdon, 2006). A Massachusetts-based information research company, Cutter Consortium, conducted a survey to identify the problems faced during development of web applications (Cutter Research Briefs, 2000).

The complexity is further enhanced by the requirement of integrating the developed web application with traditional information systems such as processing transaction, database management and other information exchange services. There is more to web application development than visual design and user interface. It involves planning, selection of an appropriate web architecture, system design, page design, coding, content creation and its maintenance, testing, quality assurance and performance evaluation. It also involves continual update and maintenance of the web system as the well as post-launch operational review of the system. To successfully build complex web-based systems and applications, both large and small, web developers need to adopt a disciplined development process and sound design methodologies and use better development tools. It can be said that simplicity is an illusion for web applications and developing them is an inherently complex and challenging task. Since the complexity of web applications is not apparent most of the web developers and project managers fail to recognize it. They develop web applications using the same approach used for traditional software development and completely ignore the multifaceted and unique requirements of web applications. The system level requirements are often overlooked and web application development is still thought of as a simple web page creation with a few hyperlinked documents. The design considerations are also ignored and so is the methodology to develop the application. Consequently, an effective

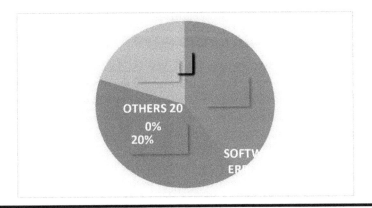

Figure 9.2   Causes of web application failures.

Source: Jazayeri, 2007

development is not achieved and results in either a poorly developed application or overestimation of budget. According to (Jazayeri, 2007), eighty percent of web applications fail due to either software or human error or vague monitoring and reporting of project's progress.

A web application failure can occur after or before launch. In case of post-launch failure, the web application fails to deliver the expected performance and functions. A more dangerous situation is failure before the launch. A web application is said to fail before launch if the development process has become very expensive and complex, or in other words 'unmanageable'. Apart from loss of revenue and tarnished reputation if the web application development process is not managed, the company also suffers from technical debt (Dong et al., 2019). Technical debt (TD) describes a situation in which a technical compromise is made, e.g., delivering not-quite-right code in order to meet an urgent deadline. A long-term loss is entrenched in the company by technical debt (Figure 9.2).

Thus, it can be concluded that a majority of web applications fail due to poor management or a complex development process. The following section discusses it in a more detailed manner.

In the second section, linear sequential models and Agile models are accessed and compared. The aim of this section is to make the reader aware about the past and current web application development methodologies and highlight the research gap.

In the third section, the proposed model is discussed and the details of all the phases of web application development are listed.

In the fourth section, the implementation of the proposed model on a project is discussed. The outcomes in terms of productivity matrix are analyzed.

The fifth and last section concludes and highlights future research directions.

9.2 Literature Review: Software Development Life Cycle

Presently, the Software Development Life Cycle (SDLC) model is used for developing web applications. The SDLC consists of the detailed plan for building and maintaining software. The different phases involved in a SDLC model are requirement gathering, requirement analysis, risk and feasibility assessment, design, coding and testing. A life cycle model when utilized in the context of web application development gives a detailed specification of the processes and deliverables in each development phase. SDLC can be either sequential or iterative.

In a sequential SDLC the requirements are gathered and freeze in the starting of the project and other development phases are taken step by step. The V model and the waterfall are some of the popular SDLC models. On the other hand, in an iterative life cycle model, the entire user requirements are not specified completely at the start of project but instead development begins with partial specification of requirements. The partial requirements are implemented and reviewed and further requirements are added. This process is then repeated, producing a new version of the software for each cycle of the model. The advantage of using the sequential approach is that it is easy to monitor and control different activities in the development, but the functionality of adapting to the changing environments and applications is lost in sequential SDLC.

Iterative SDLCs are well suited for fast changing development environments and technology. Since it is an evolutionary approach, it provides greater flexibility to the changing user requirements, and is highly beneficial especially in small and medium enterprises. However, limiting the number of iterations is a major concern while using the iterative model for developing web applications. This is because too little iteration degenerates the process into a 'build it now and fix it later' approach; on the other hand too much iteration leads to decline in efficiency of the process. Thus, it can be rightly concluded that developing a web application by iterative SDLC process is a strenuous task and requires a comprehensive management control.

Therefore traditional methodologies of developing software applications cannot ensure quality development of web applications as well. There exists immediate need to develop an iterative development life cycle model which can space specifically cater to the dynamic changing needs of application development and can ensure quality in each development phase.

9.2.1 Traditional Models

Traditional life cycle models refer to the family of development models before the development of Agile methodologies. Traditional models usually start with rigid user requirements, which cannot be changed in a lifecycle. In this section, only two popular traditional development models are discussed and compared.

9.2.1.1 Linear Sequential Model (Waterfall Model)

Royce proposed the linear sequential model in 1970 (Klopper, 2007). The linear sequential model is also called the waterfall model because it illustrates a straight and sequential software development life cycle. The different stages in a linear sequential model are requirement gathering and analysis, coding, testing and implementation. However the development process is very rigid. This means the next stage is executed only if the previous one is finished and the stage once completed is cannot be improvised. The improvisations take place only when the project is finished completely. Another important characteristic of linear sequential models is that they involve extreme documentation in all the development phases. These approaches are, therefore, also referred to as 'document-driven development models' (Figure 9.3).

Though the waterfall model is the very first software development life cycle model, it is still used in many development projects. The reason behind this is less complexity and high security since it is a document-driven process. However, the model has major drawbacks which make it unsuitable for the present situation of continuous technological evolution. Major drawbacks of waterfall model are listed here:

Once a particular stage is finished the feedback can be conveyed to the previous stages such as the feedback from implementation activity can be conveyed to design activity. Thus, the changes that impact previous activities can be accommodated (Tipaldi et al., 2016).

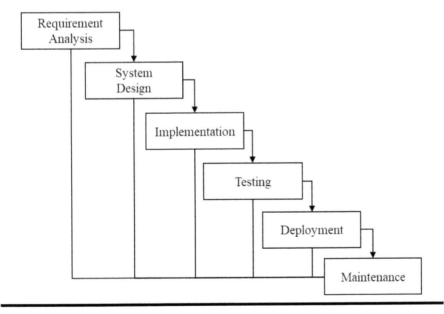

Figure 9.3   Linear sequential model.

Source: Subair, 2014

9.2.1.2 Agile Model

Agile methodology shifted the life cycle models from linear sequential flow to iterative flow. The main principle of Agile methodology is increasing efficiency and stability during the web application development procedure while maintaining quality of the web application by avoiding wastage of resources. Therefore, short iterations are involved in this process (Rasnacis et al., 2017). The different stages involved in the software development life cycle by the Agile process are requirement gathering, analysis, design, coding, testing, implementation and user feedback. In agile development, the highest priority is given to the customer satisfaction. Development time is expected to be as short as possible. The software development life cycle of the Agile process is shown in Figure 9.4 (Bhalerao, 2009). Planning is not an arduous task in Agile because the entire task is delivered in small increments. The difference between Agile development and linear sequential development is elaborated in Tables 9.1 and 9.2.

The Agile process is preferred in short-term projects which are developed with small and moderately experienced team members. In Agile, the customer is involved in each iteration this, reducing chances of failure. In the Agile process the changes can be incorporated in iterations to ensure customer satisfaction.

So, the linear sequential model and Agile development are comparable because the linear sequential model is a base model and the Agile development model is used by current industry.

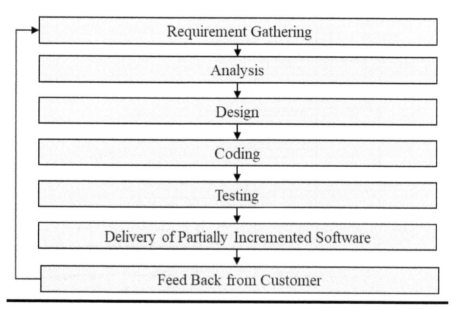

Figure 9.4   Process of Agile methodology.

Source: Bhalerao, 2009

Table 9.1   Difference between Agile Development and Linear Sequential Development

Parameters	Linear Sequential Model	Agile Model
Type	Sequential	Iterative
Principal Objectives	Optimization, predictability and repeatability	Responding to change and developing quick business value
Customers	The waterfall model requires adequately skilled and knowledgeable customers.	Agile requires dedicated, co-located, knowledgeable customers.
Relations with Customers	Customer is involved only in the requirement gathering phase.	Customer is involved dedicatedly in the entire development process.
Planning and Control	Planning is a strenuous process. Controlling and tracking the project is easy.	Rigorous planning is not required; the development can start with initial requirements and forecasts. However, the process is difficult to control due to continuous improvements.
Planning Scale	Long term	Short term
Offshore or Nearshore Customers	For offshore customers, there is a large distance between the development team and customer.	Nearshore customers are in proximity to development team.
Time between Specification and Implementation	High	Low
Project Schedule Risk	High	Low
Communication between Team	Communication through explicit documentation	Informal, face-to-face communication
Flexibility	Waterfall models have little scope for accommodating changes in requirements.	Agile has better accommodation for changing user's needs.
Development	The waterfall model relies heavily upon software architecture, since it is part of the development sequence.	Agile values working software over comprehensive documentation, and emphasizes simplicity.

(Continued)

Table 9.1 (Continued)

Parameters	Linear Sequential Model	Agile Model
Developers	Waterfall developers are to be plan-oriented, adequately skilled with access to external knowledge.	Agile project developers are to be agile, knowledgeable, collocated and collaborative, and should be amicable, talented, skillful and communicative.
Project Size	Better suited for large projects.	Better suited for small projects.
Testing Method	Highly documented and conventional quality assurance method are used. Architecture is the prime focus of testing.	Internal design and code review are used.
Testing Phase	Testing starts after development and build phases are completed.	Testing and development happen concurrently.
Test Planning	Planning the testing phase is done just before the testing phase.	The tests to be conducted are planned before starting the project.
Team	The testing team is separated from the development team by a strict line. They cannot participate in a development phase other than testing.	The testing team can participate in requirement gathering and modifications. The testing team has active communication with the development team.
Test Cases	Test cases are created in the last phase for all functionalities.	Test cases are created in each iteration.
Acceptance Testing	Performed by client after release.	Performed after each iteration by test team or business analyst; consequently, done by client after each release.
Documentation	Extensive.	Limited.
Type of Product Delivery	Massive and completed delivery at the end of development process.	Project delivered in parts, each iteration producing a minimum viable product (MVP).
Culture	Best suited for organizations and projects that have a high degree of order with clear and precise user requirements.	Best suited for organizations and project that have less order and more chaos. The requirements are not fully known and understood in starting of the project.

Table 9.2 Comparative Research to Find the Appropriate Research Gap

Year	Title	Objective	Contribution	Support for requirement elicitation	Support for standards	Support for Complexity Management	Attention to Design Activities
2010	USABAGILE_ Web: a web Agile usability approach for website design (Benigni et al., 2010)	To present an Agile methodology designed for the web, to design or reengineer a software product	Usability assessment activities (Inspection, Evaluation and Questionnaire) are incorporated in Agile methodology. The results of these activities are documented in a special usability report.	YES	NO	NO	YES
2012	A scrum-based approach to CMMI maturity level 2 in web development environments (Salinas et al., 2012)	To combine characteristics of Scrum and CMM model to benefit the organizatio ns.	An additional sprint called 'Sprint 0' at the beginning of the Scrum process is proposed which deals with quality assurance, project data management and project evaluation.	YES	NO	YES	NO

(Continued)

Table 9.2 (Continued)

Year	Title	Objective	Contribution	Support for requirement elicitation	Support for standards	Support for Complexity Management	Attention to Design Activities
2013	S-Scrum: a secure methodology for Agile development of web services (Mougouei et al., 2013)	To eliminate drawbacks of Scrum.	A security-enhanced version of Scrum, Secure Scrum (S-Scrum) is proposed to incorporate security analysis and design activities into the Scrum processes. The proposed methodology has modified the scrum processes to accommodate documentation activities which reflect the security aspects of the target web service.	NO	NO	YES	NO
2014	Mockup-Driven Development: Providing Agile support for Model-Driven Web Engineering (Rivero et al., 2014)	To propose an approach that eases the incorporation of well-known Agile practices to Model-Driven Web Engineering (MDWE) methodologies	MockupDD, an Agile model-driven web engineering methodology based on Scrum, is proposed; its process consists of four phases: mockup construction, mockup processing, features specification and tags refinement, code and model generation.	YES	NO	NO	NO

Year	Title	Objective	Contribution	Support for requirement elicitation	Support for standards	Support for Complexity Management	Attention to Design Activities
2015	A Methodology and Tool Support for Widget-Based Web Application Development (Nicolaescu and Klamma, 2015)	The aim of this paper is to reengineering approach for web applications to reduce maintenance cost and efforts and prevent outdating of the web application.	A widget-based collaborative web applications development is proposed in which the presentation layer is entirely composed of widgets to help designers in reengineering.	NO	NO	NO	YES
2015	MetaPage: A Data-Intensive MockupDD for Agile Web Engineering (Angelaccio, 2016)	The motivating reason is to have a new type of web framework which shares the advantages of mockup-driven engineering methodology with the ones of model-driven engineering approach without forcing the user to work on different tools.	Agile development is combined with classical model-driven web development process in a unique visual framework, the model is named 'Data-Intensive mockup-driven development'. The data-binding mechanisms are employed to generate an automatic UML model.	NO	NO	NO	YES

(Continued)

Table 9.2 (Continued)

Year	Title	Objective	Contribution	Support for requirement elicitation	Support for standards	Support for Complexity Management	Attention to Design Activities
2017	SXP: Simplified extreme programing process model (Anwer and Aftab, 2017)	To overcome the limitations of extreme programming. Lack of documentation, poor architectural structure and less focus on design are its major drawbacks that affect the performance of extreme programming.	A modified version of XP called simplified extreme programing (SXP) is proposed that eliminates some complexities of XP such as pair programming to simplify XP without affecting its agility. The various phases are explained without adequate details and the validation is also missing.	NO	NO	NO	NO
2017	A Supporting Tool for Requirements Change Management in Distributed Agile Development (Lloyd et al., 2017)	To develop a tool to manage requirements and their changes during the distributed agile development processes.	A novel feature model called the feature tree is introduced. The tool helps to manage the requirement changes and helps the project manager to keep track of project status at the two phases.	NO	NO	NO	NO

Year	Title	Objective	Contribution	Support for requirement elicitation	Support for standards	Support for Complexity Management	Attention to Design Activities
2018	An Agile and Collaborative Model-Driven Development Framework for Web Applications (Romano and Cunha, 2018)	To increase the productivity in web application development by reducing efforts to model the system and inconsistencies in the requirements gathering stage.	AC-MDD framework that helps maintain consistency within system's requirements and generating process. In the proposed framework a detailed modeling of requirements is performed before the design phase.	YES	NO	NO	NO
2018	Model-Based Rapid Prototyping and Evolution of Web Application (Falzone and Bernaschina, 2018)	To counteract the problems of model-driven development forward engineering when manual and automatic code updates occur in parallel.	An online tool for rapid prototyping of web applications is demonstrated. The tool develops a prototype of the web application and helps in studying the user interaction with the web application. In other words different variations of an application can be developed in a short time period by rapidly modifying the application model and generating realistic prototypes, easily turned into deployable applications.	NO	NO	YES	YES

It can be said that the process of web application development is a complex and multidisciplinary approach. Despite the large number of existing approaches, they essentially concentrate on development phases and do not cover other areas like project estimation, quality assurance or team management.

From the reviewed literature it can be said that the process of web application development is a complex and multidisciplinary approach. Despite the large number of existing approaches, they essentially concentrate on development phases and do not cover other areas like project estimation, quality assurance or team management.

Technical debt management is a neglected issue and a dedicated research is required to identify and test the practices which can prevent technical debt.

The existing Agile development models are not capable of assisting teams in gathering the correct or the actual requirement and scope of the web application from the client.

9.3 Proposed Iterative Lifecycle Model

The proposed iterative lifecycle model for development of web applications is drafted after a careful study of the problems faced by organizations while developing web applications and the possible solutions for the same.

The proposed model is named 'Agile with Requirement and Quality Inspection (ARQI)' as the emphasis during the development cycles on maintaining quality in each phase and correct interpretation of client requirements. The proposed model for web application development is different from traditional approaches in many aspects. The distinctive features of the proposed model are as follows:

- Inclusion of requirement and quality inspector (RQI)
- Design according to standards
- Quality gateway for coding
- Checking for scope creep and domino effect in subsequent iterations

One factor of novelty is the inclusion of a **requirement and quality inspector (RQI).** During the literature review and analysis of conducted surveys it was found that a large number of iterations result because of unclear requirement gathering. The client generally has a vague idea about the requirements. Expectation mismatch occurs even after drafting of SRS. The effect of the unclear requirement objectives gets magnified during the design phase. The requirement and quality inspector is a technical professional whose responsibilities are as follows:

- To gather pragmatic requirements from client and clearly communicate it to the team

- To provide a secondary review in the design phase and decrease the chances of expectation mismatch
- To check the changes suggested by the client for scope creep and domino effect in subsequent iterations

The proposed model is schematically represented in Figure 9.5. The web application development starts with pragmatic requirement gathering. In this stage the requirements from the client are gathered by the project manager in the presence of the RQI. The term 'pragmatic' is associated with requirement gathering because instead of beginning with vague requirements from the client, the RQI tries to extract the actual requirements by defining the actual scope of the web application and discussing the same with the client. Once the requirements are finalized, requirement analysis is done and the result is a software resource specification (SRS), which consists of all the functional and nonfunctional requirements.

The next stage is 'design with standards'. At this stage the appearance and structure design take place but by adhering to the design standards. The design standards ensure avoidance of common design mistakes by moderately experienced developers and thus preventing unnecessary iterations. Once the design is finalized, it is passed to the RQI for review. This stage is included to ensure a centralized control

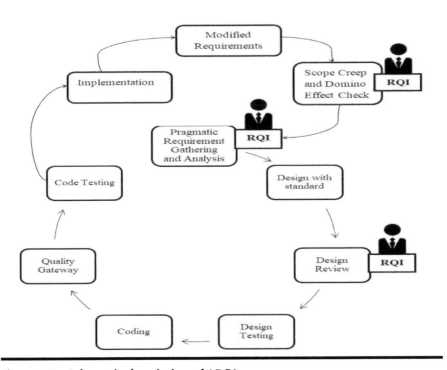

Figure 9.5   Schematic description of ARQI.

of expectation matching, because the RQI is in direct communication with the client; if he finds expectation mismatch, the previous stage is repeated. However, if the RQI does not find any flaws, then the design is tested and errors are rectified.

In the next stage the backend development takes place and a source code is formed. The source code is firstly passed through a quality gateway to ensure that code is sufficient in quality in order to avoid complications in code testing. In the next stage of code testing the source code is checked for errors by code testing technologies such as unit testing. Once the bugs are removed the entire web application is tested in the next stage called 'testing'. The web application is tested for functionality, usability, performance, database, compatibility and security. After testing the next stage is implementation. In this stage the web application is deployed on local server and the changes are identified. The changes demanded by the client are first checked for scope creep and domino effect by the RQI. If it is found that the changes are conflicting with the scope of the web application and requires significant efforts, then the changes are modified or dropped after discussing with the client.

ARQI ensures that quality is maintained in each phase of development and changes are easier to implement by ensuring designing with standards and testing code for quality as well. With ARQI, scope creep and domino effect can be reduced.

The proposed model is applied to web application development. The proposed framework has certain limitations, as listed later.

The proposed model is defined in a generic way and is not extensively documented. To do the same requires explicit details of all the aspects of a commercial web application which cannot be provided immediately.

9.3.1 Proposed Model

In this section, the different phases of the proposed iterative model for web application development are discussed in detail.

9.3.1.1 Pragmatic Requirement Gathering

Identifying users' needs is the foremost step in the project induction. In a traditional Agile methodology, the client sends his initial requirements to the project manager related to the project. The development team is required to break down the requirements into the scope of work. For instance, in Scrum, the requirements are broken into disparate buckets of work wherein the largest buckets are called Epics (defining the major items of development). The Epics are further divided into smaller pieces of work called Stories, which are further split into individual tasks. While planning the project under Agile, one has to carefully consider the dependencies between each of the Epics and Stories. The tasks are then prioritized depending on the business demands. Finally, the Epics and Stories are slotted into blocks of development time, called Sprints, for development.

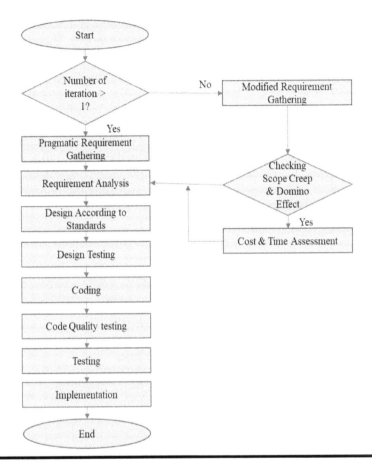

Figure 9.6   Detailed description of ARQI.

In the proposed model, the RQI is involved in discussion with the client along with the project manager while gathering requirements (Figure 9.6). In the initial communication with the client, the RQI and project manager are required to form a clear and precise answer to the following questions:

- Why is the web application being developed?
- Who are the target users?
- What does the organization expect from the website?
- Once the aforementioned queries are resolved, the RQI is required to accomplish the following tasks:
- Capture as many details from inception so that there is less rework, more preparedness and more clarity.
- Match expectations between different stakeholders.

As a result, even though the web application looks assuring and attractive, it might not be able cater to individual user needs, goals and expectations. These lacunae lead to increased costs and maintenance problems in the project. Web applications need all the more attention here because of heterogeneous customers, dynamic behavior and vast reach in contrast to the traditional applications, in which the users are known and their expectations can be easily captured.

The process flow to be followed in requirement gathering phase is shown in Figure 9.7. Firstly, initial client's requirements are gathered. The requirements are then elicited and the details are drawn by the RQI, and the RQI finds some conflict of interest or goals. The client is educated about the conflicting expectations, and suitable modifications are suggested by the RQI. These modifications, if approved by the client, are passed to the requirement analysis phase.

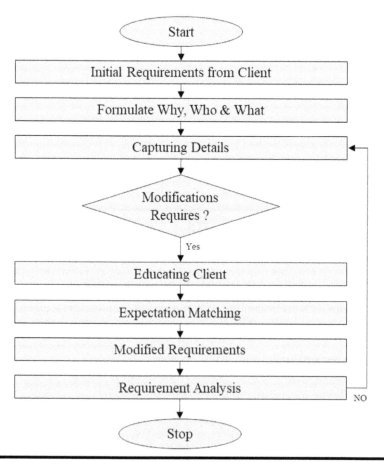

Figure 9.7   Process flow for requirement gathering phase.

9.3.1.2 Requirement Analysis

Once the requirements are gathered the cost–benefit analysis is performed in the requirement analysis phase, the objectives are analyzed for feasibility. The objective of this phase is to ensure that the requirements are clear, complete and unambiguous. In this phase the shared understanding between the different stakeholders is developed and it becomes clear: 'What is going to be developed?'

The process flow of this stage is shown in Figure 9.8. Firstly, the functional and non-functional requirements of the project are drafted. The required frontend and backend technologies are also listed. The project manager then performs the cost analysis and estimates the total project cost or effort. The next step is risk assessment and feasibility analysis. If the project is feasible a software requirement specification

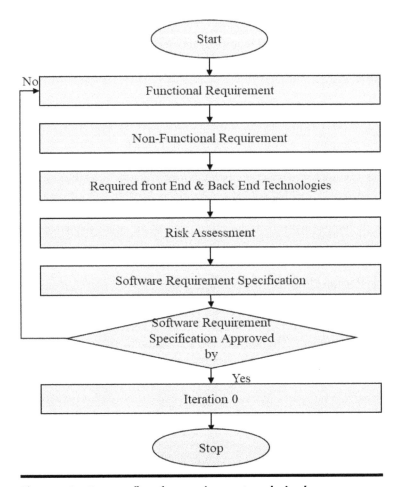

Figure 9.8 **Process flow for requirement analysis phase.**

(SRS) is drafted and sent to the client for approval. If the SRS is approved by the client then iteration 0 is initiated. The aforementioned terms are discussed briefly in the following section.

9.3.1.2.1 Functional Requirements

The requirements which are responsible for technical functionality of the system are called functional requirements. Functional requirements define the interaction of users with the web application. They denote the actions that an application must be able to perform and they must be testable.

9.3.1.2.2 Non-Functional Requirements

The criteria used for judging the operation of the web application in particular conditions is specified by non-functional requirements. Instead of defining specific behaviors, non-functional requirements specify how the system is supposed to behave. In other words non-functional requirements define the quality attributes of a system.

9.3.1.2.3 Required Frontend Technologies

Frontend is the part of a web-based system with which user interacts. Frontend is also called the 'client side' of the application. It includes all the elements of direct user interaction such as navigation menu, buttons, graphs and tables, text style and colors. The languages which are used in frontend development are JavaScript, CSS and HTML. The frontend developers are responsible for planning and implementing the structure, content, behavior and design of all visual elements in the web-based system.

9.3.1.2.4 Required Backend Technologies

The server side of the web-based system is referred as 'backend'. The objective of backend is to ensure that the client side is working correctly by appropriately storing and arranging data. The user cannot interact with this part of a web site or web application. Backend technologies refer to the software which is essential for the correct functioning of web-based systems but are not in direct contact with the users.

9.3.1.2.5 Cost Analysis

In cost analysis the total cost required for project completion is predicted. The total cost is the sum of system costs, design costs, learning costs and implementation costs.

9.3.1.2.6 Risk Assessment

In this step the project manager drafts the probable risks and their intensity. The risks such as tendency of over and underestimation of time and cost, etc., are formulated and it is decided if the project is feasible or not.

9.3.1.2.7 Software Requirements Specification (SRS)

The document containing a detailed description of the web application to be developed, containing all functional and non-functional requirements, is known as a software requirements specification (SRS). The SRS is drafted based on the agreements between various stakeholders. A good SRS clearly defines all the necessary requirements for project development such as the type of human–computer interaction, internal modules, communications, hardware and other programs.

9.3.1.2.7.1 Iteration 0   Iteration 0 meetings are a conversation between stakeholders and the team before the first iteration of a release. This ensures the team is ready with people, process and tools in order to begin making progress in iterations.

9.3.1.3 Design With Standards

In any web application, design is a crucial factor that determines its success. In this phase both appearance and structure design take place. The structure design usually represents the network of hyperlinks that makes navigating the web site feasible and simple. In appearance design, the look and feel of the web site are finalized, keeping in mind the end-users and requirements of the client. To reduce the number of iterations, we have specified some standards for design as mentioned in the following. These standards not only reduce the number of iterations but can also help designers to avoid common design mistakes.

9.3.1.3.1 Adding Unnecessary Design Elements

Developers, often less experienced ones, pay immense attention towards the aesthetic characteristics of a web application and try to incorporate unique graphic elements. These elements often have no functional use and unnecessarily complicate the user experience. The objective of this standard is to remind the developer that usability is priority over aesthetic appeal.

9.3.1.3.2 Restricted Number of Colors and Typefaces

The web application must be designed with minimum 3 and maximum 7 colors. The typefaces used must be legible; customized typefaces, which are not compatible with every browser environment, must not be used unless necessary. The typefaces should not be of more than three colors. The design must follow a common color theme.

9.3.1.3.3 Visual Hierarchy

Position, size and color of crucial elements, such as click-to-action buttons, must be structured in a manner that establishes visual hierarchy. Visual hierarchy is a must to ensure that the attention of user is automatically drawn to the most important elements in a natural way.

9.3.1.3.4 Easy Navigability

Since the users are visiting a lot of web applications a familiar navigation scheme must be followed. The navigation must not be complicated, and the user must know where to click next without excessive thought. The navigation symbols should not be too customized and must be recognizable. Navigation should be placed at footers and search tabs on the top right corner. Breadcrumbs must be used where appropriate. The navigation must be consistent on all pages.

9.3.1.3.5 Using Flexible Structure

The web application must be designed keeping in mind the accessibility parameter. This suggests compatibility with different browsers and devices. Therefore a flexible structure such as responsive design must be adopted.

9.3.1.4 Design Review

Once a design is finalized it is reviewed by the requirement and quality inspector since he is in direct contact with the client and can convey the expectations of the client clearly. If the requirement and quality inspector finds expectation mismatch, he can again send the design to the previous phase for improvement.

9.3.1.5 Design Testing

Once the design is approved by the RQI it is passed to design testing phase. Testing design early is very important to avoid blunders in the last stage. In this phase both the structure and appearance of the design are tested for functionality, and if some discrepancy is found, the design is again sent back to the design phase.

9.3.1.6 Coding

In this phase, the backend coding is performed. For this firstly requirements are gathered. The requirements may be databases, staff training repository, technical specifications and software. After gathering the requirements, the designer converts the design into machine code. The output of the stage is the finalized design document.

9.3.1.7 Code Quality Testing

Once the coding has been performed it passes through a quality gateway in the proposed model. Traditionally the subsequent phase after coding is testing. However, in the proposed model an additional phase is allocated 'to test code for quality'. The objective of this phase is to restrict bad coding practices to ensure a code that is both easy to read and testable.

9.4 Implementation and Results

The proposed iterative lifecycle model by the name 'Agile with Requirement and Quality Inspection (ARQI)' is implemented during development of a web application based on the Internet of Things (IOT). The application was developed within Tishitu, a part of MNIT Innovation and Incubation Centre, Jaipur, India. The authorities agreed to provide an insight of the development process being used in their organization through a pilot experiment. Additionally, the authorities also agreed to test the proposed model by implementing it on an additional pilot experiment.

9.4.1 Case Study for ARQI

In this case study the web application is developed using ARQI. The details of the case study are mentioned according to the minutes of the meeting between the RQI, team leader, team and/or client. The time period for each iteration was short and usually each iteration lasted for twelve days. The team comprises:

- Team leader
- RQI
- Designer
- Coder
- Tester

Table 9.3   Initial Forecast or Iteration 0 Estimates Case Study for ARQI

INITIAL FORECAST	
Number of story points	56
Total available hours	654
Hours per story point	10.9
Planned working hours per iteration	119
Predicted number of iterations	4
Initial team velocity (predicted in story points)	15
Cost per iteration	50,000 INR
Uncertainty	±16%

The number of story points to be completed is 56. The predicted number of iterations is 4. Each iteration should not last for more than 200 hours. There are 119 planned working hours in each iteration (Table 9.3).

9.4.1.1 Data Analysis

The major figures of the project are shown in Table 9.4. Based on these figures the Earned Value Metrics is formed as shown in Table 9.5. The parameters used for EVM are Team Velocity (TV), Work Capacity (WC), Focus Factor (FF), Target Value Increase (TVI+), Expected Percent Completed (EPC), Actual Percent Completed (EPC), Planned Value (PV) and Earned Value (EV). The project started

Table 9.4   Major Figures of Project

Iteration	1	2	3	4	5
Start Date	03/06/19	15/06/19	27/06/19	07/06/19	17/06/19
End Date	14/06/19	26/06/19	06/07/19	16/07/19	28/07/19
Working Days	12	12	12	12	12
Estimated Velocity	15	11	16	16	14
Real Velocity	7	10	10	17	14
Finished Story Points	7	17	27	44	58
Backlog Story Points	56	56	59	58	58
Remaining Story Points	49	32	32	14	0
Estimated Working Hours	119	119	119	119	119
Real Working Hours	60	70	60	59	60

Table 9.5   Earned Value Metrics of Project

Iteration	1	2	3	4	5
AH/SP	10.9	10.9	10.9	10.9	10.9
Work Capacity	119	119	119	119	119
Team Velocity	65.4	109	109	196.2	152.6
Focus Factor	60	81.9	64.68	87.5	78
TVI+	0.62	0.89	0.89	1.52	1.25
EPC	0.27	0.32	0.55	0.74	1
APC	0.125	0.3	0.46	0.76	1
PV	67,500	80,000	1,37,500	1,85,500	2,50,000
EV	31,250	75,000	1,15,000	1,90,000	2,50,000

with 56 story points; 3 story points were added in third iteration and 1 story point was removed in fourth iteration. The project burn-up chart is shown in Figure 9.9. It can be seen that the development proceeded with fewer fluctuations in number of story points. Other important aspects of the development with ARQI are explained with Figure 9.10–9.13.

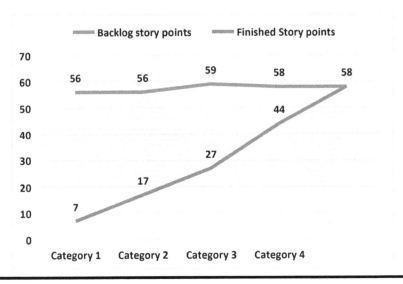

Figure 9.9   Project burn-up chart.

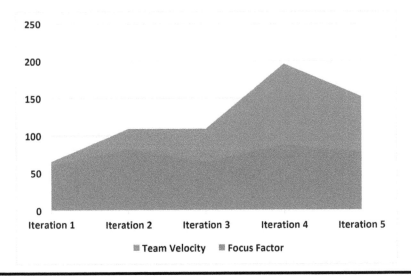

Figure 9.10   Trend of team velocity and focus factor in project.

From Figure 9.10 it can be observed that the project started with less team velocity which increased in subsequent iterations. The focus factor also has a positive growth trend and mostly remained greater than 100, thus denoting an efficient team. The TVI+ also showed a positive growth trend, as can be seen from Figure 9.11.

The relation between EPC and APC can be seen in Figure 9.12. It can be seen that APC closely follows the trend of EPC. A similar relation is observed between PV and EV in Figure 9.13. This signifies that the deviations in the project from planned or estimated parameters are less than expected.

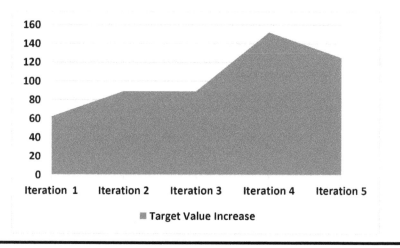

Figure 9.11   Trend of target value increase in project.

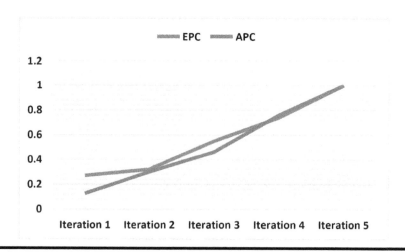

Figure 9.12   Estimated percent complete (EPC) versus actual percent completed (APC).

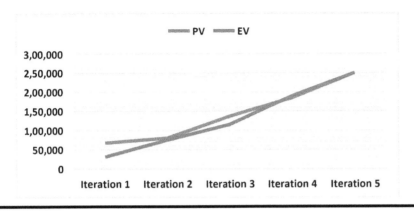

Figure 9.13 Planned value versus earned value (EV).

9.4.1.2 Observations

- The project was completed with increased client and team satisfaction.
- A minor percentage of underestimation (20%) was found.
- Coordination between the different stages of development improved because of the presence of an RQI, who acted as a collaborating channel.
- The number of iterations and the time in iterations was reduced. Since the design was according to standards, changes were possible even with switching of team members.
- Some minor managerial issues arose due to inclusion of an RQI.

9.4.2 Case Study for Scrum

In this case study Scrum was used for web application development. The company prefers using Scrum for most of its development projects. The details of the case study are presented according to the minutes of sprint meetings in presence of the Scrum master. The team comprises:

- Team leader
- Scrum master
- Designer
- Coder
- Tester

Role of Scrum vs RQI: The Scrum master is the team role responsible for ensuring the team lives Agile values and principles and follows the processes and practices that the team agreed they would use. On the other hand, an RQI acts as a central monitoring person. The RQI is responsible for client education to prevent scope creep, quality assurance and technical debt prevention (Figures 9.14 to 9.18 and Tables 9.6 to 9.8).

Table 9.6   Initial Forecast Case Study for Scrum

INITIAL FORECAST	
Number of story points	48
Total available hours	654
Hours per story point	13.6
Planned working hours per iteration	116
Predicted number of iterations	4
Initial team velocity (predicted in story points)	11
Cost per iteration	50,000 INR
Uncertainty	±16%

Table 9.7   Major Points Case Study for Scrum

Sprint	1	2	3	4	5	6
Start Date	03/06/19	15/06/19	27/06/19	7/06/19	17/06/19	29/07/19
End Date	14/06/19	26/06/19	6/07/19	16/07/19	28/07/19	12/08/19
Working Days	12	12	12	12	12	12
Estimated Velocity	1	11	16	15	14	12
Real Velocity	9	10	4	8	10	12
Finished Story Points	9	19	30	38	52	64
Backlog Story Points	45	45	60	65	64	64
Remaining Story Points	36	26	30	22	12	0
Estimated Working Hours	111	111	111	111	111	111
Real Working Hours	12	12	12	12	12	12

Table 9.8   Performance Metric Case Study for Scrum

Iteration	AH/SP	WC	TV	FF	TVI+	EPC	APC	PV	EV
1	13.6	116	97.2	83	0.83	0.24	0.20	72,000/-	60,000/-
2	13.6	116	205.2	176	1.76	0.44	0.42	132,000/-	1,26,000/-
3	13.6	116	43.2	37	0.37	0.58	0.50	1,74,000/-	1,50,000/-
4	13.6	116	86.4	74	0.74	0.69	0.58	2,07,000/-	1,74,000/-
5	13.6	116	151.2	130	0.925	0.81	0.81	2,43,000/-	2,43,000/-
6	13.6	116	140.4	130	1.11	1	1	3,00,000/-	3,00,000/-

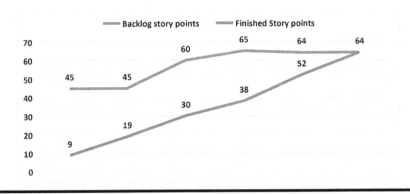

Figure 9.14   Project burn-up chart case study for Scrum.

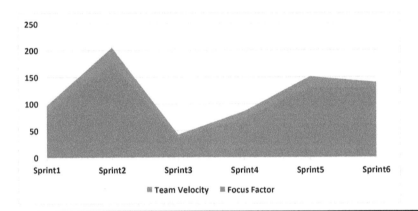

Figure 9.15   Trend of team velocity and focus factor case study for Scrum.

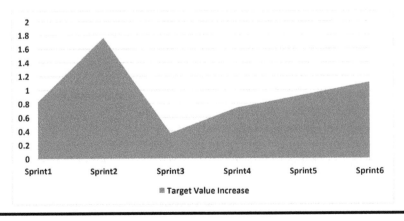

Figure 9.16   Trend of target value increase in case study for Scrum.

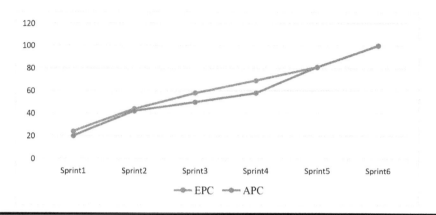

Figure 9.17 **EPC versus APC case study for Scrum.**

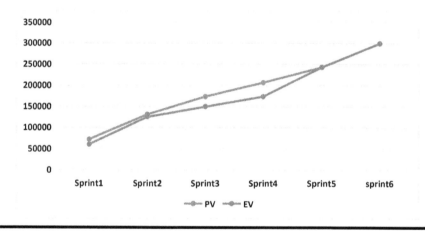

Figure 9.18 **PV versus EV case study for Scrum.**

9.4.2.1 Observations

- Due to large number of advertisements, the application took longer to load.
- The customized fonts created compatibility issues.
- The end user experience was not as expected.
- The actual effort exceeded the predicted effort by 15% with increased entropy in management and technical teams.

The comparison of performance matrix obtained by Scrum and ARQI is mentioned in Table 9.9. Both the projects started with similar resources and available hours. The ARQI process advanced with higher initial velocity (Figures 9.19 and 9.20).

Table 9.9   Comparison of Productivity Matrices of ARQI and Scrum

Parameters	ARQI	Scrum
Available hours	600	600
Average hours per use case	10.9	13.58
Initial story points	56	45
Initial velocity (team velocity in first iteration)	15	11
Average team velocity	126.44	120.6
Average work capacity	119	116
Average focus factor	106.25	103.38
Average target value increase	103.4	95.55
Predicted deviation	±16%	±16%
Actual deviation	+20%	+31%

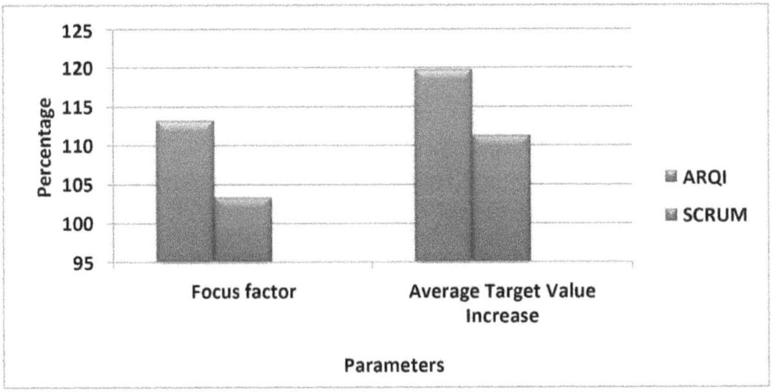

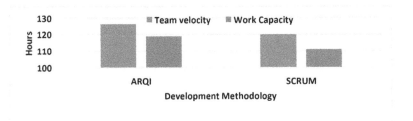

Figure 9.19   Comparison of focus factor and TVI+ delivered by ARQI and Scrum.

Figure 9.20   Relationship between team velocity and work capacity in ARQI and Scrum.

The ARQI process advanced with higher initial velocity due to additional time invested in client education. However, team velocity increased in subsequent iterations. It can be observed that ARQI, though slow in initial stages, shows better productivity value with increased focus factor and target value increase. Due to quality assurance in each development phase, the average hours in each iteration are less as compared to Scrum.

9.5 Conclusions

A new life cycle model for web application called 'Agile with Requirement and Quality Inspection (ARQI)' is developed to ensure pragmatic requirement gathering and assuring quality in all development phases. The proposed model was validated by practical implementation in a case study. The results show that the proposed model provides better earned value management (EVM) in web application development.

9.6 Future Scope

The proposed the identification of technical debt and scope creep are based on subjective analysis of a requirement and quality inspector (RQI). This aspect can be further enhanced by automating it, using innovative technologies of artificial intelligence and machine learning.

References

Angelaccio, M. (2016) 'MetaPage-a data intensive MockupDD for agile web engineering', in Helfert, M. (ed.) *12th International Conference on Web Information Systems and Technologies.* Webist, pp. 315–317.

Anwer, F. and Aftab, S. (2017) 'SXP: simplified extreme programing process model', *International Journal of Modern Education and Computer Science*, 9(6), p. 25.

Benigni, G., Gervasi, O., Passeri, F. L. and Kim, T. H. (2010) 'USABAGILE_Web: A web agile usability approach for web site design'. In *Computational Science and Its Applications– ICCSA 2010: International Conference*, Fukuoka, Japan, March 23–26, 2010, Part II 10 (pp. 422–431). Springer Berlin Heidelberg.

Bhalerao, S., Puntambekar, D. and Ingle, M. (2009) 'Generalizing agile software development life cycle'. *International Journal on Computer Science and Engineering*, 1(3), pp. 222–226.

Cutter Research Briefs (2000) *Cutter consortium, poor project management number-one problem of outsourced eprojects.* Available at: www.cutter.com/article/poor-project-management-number-one-problem- outsourced-e-projects-430456 (accessed 8 March 2016).

Dong, Q. H., Ocker, F. and Vogel-Heuser, B. (2019) 'Technical debt as indicator for weaknesses in engineering of automated production systems'. *Production Engineering*, 13, pp. 273–282.

Falzone, E. and Bernaschina, C. (2018) 'Model based rapid prototyping and evolution of web application', in Mikkonen, T., Klamma, R., and Hernandez, J. (eds.) *International Conference on Web Engineering*. Cham: Springer, pp. 496–500.

Jazayeri, M. (2007) 'Some trends in web application development' in Lionel, C. (ed.) *Future of Software Engineering*. Minneapolis, MN: IEEE, pp. 199–213.

Klopper, R.,Gruner, S. and Kourie, D. (2007) 'Assessment of a framework to compare software development methodologies', in Barnard, L. and Botha, R. A.(eds.). *Annual Research Conference of the South African Institute of Computer Scientists and Information Technologists on IT Research in Developing Countries*. New York: ACM, pp. 56–65.

Lloyd, D., Moawad, R. and Kadry, M. (2017) 'A supporting tool for requirements change management in distributed agile development', *Future Computing and Informatics Journal*, 2(1), pp. 1–9.

Mougouei, D., Sani, N.F.M. and Almasi, M.M. (2013) 'S-scrum: a secure methodology for agile development of web services', *World of Computer Science and Information Technology Journal (WCSIT)*, 3(1), pp. 15–19.

Nicolaescu, P. and Klamma, R. (2015) 'A methodology and tool support for widget-based web application development', in Cimiano, P., Frasincar, F., Houben, G. and Schwabe, D. (eds.) *International Conference on Web Engineering*. Cham: Springer, pp. 515–532.

Okanovic,V. (2014) 'Web application development with component frameworks', in Biljanovic, P.Z. and Gros, S. (eds.) *37th International Convention on Information and Communication Technology*. Croatia: IEEE, pp. 889–892.

Rasnacis, A. and Berzisa, S. (2017) 'Method for adaptation and implementation of agile project management methodology', *Procedia Computer Science*, 104, pp. 43–50.

Rivero, J.M., Grigera, J., Rossi, G., Luna, E.R., Montero, F. and Gaedke, M. (2014) 'Mockup-driven development: providing agile support for model-driven web engineering', *Information and Software Technology*, 56(6), pp. 670–687.

Romano, B.L. and Cunha, A.M. (2018) 'An agile and collaborative model-driven development framework for web applications', in Latifi, S. (ed.) *Information Technology-New Generations*. Cham: Springer, pp. 383–394.

Salinas, C.T., Escalona, M.J. and Mejías, M. (2012) 'A scrum-based approach to CMMI maturity level 2 in web development environments', in Taniar, D., Pardede, E., Steinbauer, M. and Khalil, I. (eds.) *Proceedings of the 14th International Conference on Information Integration and Web-based Applications & Services*. Cham: Springer, pp. 282–285.

Subair, S. (2014) 'The evolution of software process models: from the waterfall model to the unified modelling language (UML)', *International Journal of Information Technology & Systems*, 3(2), pp. 7–14.

Tipaldi, M., Ferraguto, M., Moellmann, C. and Bruenjes, B. (2016, June) A robust development process for space SW projects. In *2016 IEEE Metrology for Aerospace (MetroAeroSpace)* (pp. 348–352). IEEE.

Verdon, D. (2006) 'Security policies and the software developer', *IEEE Security & Privacy*, 4(4), pp. 42–49.

Williams, J. (2001) 'Avoiding the CNN moment', *IT Professional*, 3(2), pp. 72–70.

Chapter 10

The Future Possibilities of Artificial Intelligence in Modern Drapes

Ishwinder Kaur and Sambaditya Raj

10.1 Introduction

For everyone in the fashion business, comprising designers, producers, retailers, stylists, and of course customers, technology is altering the protocols of the game. The use of computer technology to assist in the design of garment goods is known as "apparel CAD technology." Fashion firms cannot resist the inevitable integration of information technology, which has become a highly hot subject in the clothing sector in recent years. AI in fashion market research estimates that global spending on AI in fashion will increase from US$229 million in 2019 to US$1.26 billion by 2024, a CAGR of 40.8%. Although the digitalization of the design process in the fashion business has been slightly slower than in many other industries, modern fashion designers have merged both analogue and digital design techniques, which are fundamentally altering the fashion industry (Easters, 2012; Siersema, 2015).

The fashion industry is one of the largest industries in the world, accounting for 2% of total global GDP (about $3 trillion). According to the latest Indian Brand Equity Foundation (IBEF) study, the textile industry is a thriving sector in India valued at around US$108 billion and expected to reach US$223 billion by the end of 2021. Modern innovations like blockchain and virtual reality offer a wide range of applications in the traditional fashion industry, enabling methods of manufacturing and distribution to develop as quickly as fashion tastes and trends, which are always changing. Key fabric features and drape characteristics

DOI: 10.1201/9781003441601-10

affect how clothes look. Draping has a significant role in the visual aspect of the garment and has an impact on fit and comfort. The interplay between mechanical (tensile strength, bending, and shear) and physical (weight, thickness, yarn density, and count) features of the textiles, and the weave of the fabric type, determine the drape of the fabric and, as a result, the forms and look of the garments. Because of this, there is a crucial characteristic to take into account when selecting a fabric for a certain garment design and its intended function. To create effective mechanical simulation models that can faithfully mimic certain mechanical features, a lot of research has been done, and the particle-based physical technique is now commonly used for the virtual prototyping of clothing. Studies have also demonstrated that when realistic 3D virtual models of the human body are completely taken into account to imitate garment look and fit, garment draping simulations may be successful. Numerous researches have looked at the drape behavior of materials with various circumferential and circular seams in terms of drape coefficient and the number of folds. When applied to virtual avatars, Lim and Istook's (2011) research looked at how fabric characteristics affected draping simulations and the appearance of virtual clothing.

The introduction of digital technology has forced us to think and work in new ways to boost fashion design's capacity for innovation and change design methodologies. Fashionable clothing can become more flexible and variable as a result of the widespread use of digital technologies in our everyday lives, which can change the materials that make up their components into wholly new ones. In the future, fashion materials, according to Quinn (2012), will be fluid rather than solid and will respond, alter, and adapt to pre-programmed sets of criteria. Screen-based dynamic fashion apparel (i.e., video mapping projections) that is designed virtually or virtual-physically utilizing certain digital apps or computer software can be considered the aesthetic and expressive result of dynamic fashion design in virtual space. Virtual essentially refers to "digital," which is active or simulated on a computer or computer network. Dynamic textiles that blend virtual and physical media, like augmented or mixed-reality technology, have gained popularity during the past five years.

From the design stage to the retail shelf, technology is currently automating or enhancing every aspect of business, allowing for speedier production, more effective inventory management, and a greater range of items. All of this will lead to a more flexible industry with more options than before. In response to consumers' growing need for hyper-personalized products and experiences that also satisfy their desire for sustainability, firms will increasingly be able to provide innovative production techniques, distribution methods, raw materials, and even textiles and raw materials. The fashion sector may lose jobs to automation, however, in addition to creating entirely new jobs in engineering, customer service, and curation. As technology becomes increasingly customized, you may anticipate that more and more components of the designer and branding role will change from trend-setter to taste-interpreter. Fashion companies of all sizes and shapes utilize technology to

Figure 10.1   The present and future of AI in design.

Source: Adapted from toptal design blog www.toptal.com/designers/product-design/infographic-ai-in-design

understand and anticipate market demand and respond quickly with cutting-edge designs and adaptable trends (Figure 10.1).

Artificial intelligence will change how organizations approach product design and development with a focus on forecasting what customers will want to wear next. But algorithms won't take the position of human designers any time soon. If design house trials have taught us anything, it's that human engagement is essential for capturing AI insights and turning them into fashionable, wearable apparel. Recent works on fabrics and clothing with technological integration frequently stress their potential for artistic expression and creative experimentation in addition to their technical aspects. For instance, research on thermochromic inks and high-performance conductive materials that alter the colors, textures, and forms of textiles has been done for dynamic garment and textile applications (Berzowska and Coelho, 2005; Orth, 2004; Robertson et al., 2008; Worbin, 2010). Recent researchers have also shown social trends toward the acceptability of digital apparel and technology (Devendorf et al., 2016; Koo et al., 2014; Mackey et al., 2017a, 2017b, 2019; Tomico et al., 2017).

10.2 Review of Literature

10.2.1 "Create" a Representation/Design Visualization/ Virtual Try-On for Consumption

Virtual try-on (VTO) and augmented reality (AR) will improve and enrich the experience-consuming technique since they provide users the opportunity to view a live physical presence for the simulation of the garment or to modify their bodies to improve the fit (Delamore & Sweeney, 2010). Additionally, 3D textile simulation engines that are used to illustrate how a 2D textile pattern as seen in a CAD software system can demonstrate the characteristics of the textile, such as how stretchy, thick, fine, or flowing the material is on the body, have greatly improved the visual representation of how the fabric drapes and moves with the body (D'Apuzzo, 2007). The client may receive advice from the actual or virtual tailor or stylist, who is frequently used in online shopping platforms or kiosks, on the fit, color, and style of the clothing (Ross, 2009, 2012).

Additionally, virtual mannequins are presently being used with this technological simulation technique. Numerous other businesses now provide comparable systems. Optitex was one of the earliest widely used systems. Everyone may alter the current mannequin to represent actual anthropometrical data, which is subsequently transformed into a virtual representation of the essential human shape (D'Apuzzo, 2007). Avatars that replicate competent work on screen and can be evaluated without having to visit the retail location may be created by integrating body forms and sizes from the 3D scanned visual picture with CAD design software. Measurements done manually or digitally using virtual fitting technologies

Figure 10.2 How tech could automate fashion design.

Source: Adapted from www.cbindsights.com

decrease the amount of labor the client must do, increase the accuracy of size and fit, and save costs (Apeagyei, 2010). This combines the C of "create" with the C of "consume," enabling entrepreneurs and creative fashion managers to establish new company models and income sources. These elements in Figure 10.2 will be discussed and expanded upon concerning new business models for the fashion industry.

The purpose of augmented reality (AR) is to add digital data to the real environment, which improves the retail experience by fusing the real and the fantastical. Until now, luxury companies have viewed this as having a fashionable effect. It has a place in bespoke/high-end menswear as an alternate way to see the item on the customer without needing them to be there for the fitting. This tactic could alleviate the worry regarding scanning technologies, that Delamore and Sweeney (2010) noted.

10.2.2 Fit Preferences

Ideally, functional work attire should be simple to modify to provide various garment microclimates and permit mobility of the extremities. If clothing allows the user to move freely without feeling pressured or tense, they will likely feel comfortable. If clothing can move with the individual and the user does not need to work against the garment, the individual can perform tasks more effectively than if the clothing restricts movement (Tao et al., 2018).

The working movements were classified into the four body positions most often as their working postures: Looking Up with Arms Raised 90° in a Standing Pose, Looking Up with Arms Raised 180° in a Very Standing Pose, Bending the Torso 90° from a Standing Pose, and in a Crouched Sitting Pose. These test items were developed from observations, from a study of the functional design process of a coverall for the development of mobility.

According to Geršak (2002), the elements which determine the standard of fit are directly related to the mechanical properties of the material which influence the aesthetic drape and the 3D shape. Yu et al. (2004) commented that due to the complexities involved in fit analysis, studies supporting live models were confined to limited sample size.

Studies on the effectiveness of a 3D garment simulation as a replacement for a physical prototype have shown that it can save time and labor during the production of clothing prototypes. Prior research on 3D virtual garment simulation has concentrated on end-user assessments and buying choices or on physical measurements of correctness (Ancutiene, 2014; Kim and LaBat, 2013). To enable fitting and fit evaluation within the context of the apparel development process, Porterfield and Lamar (2017) investigated the extent to which a 3D virtual garment simulation provided functional realism, laying the groundwork for how the interactive process of garment fitting might be impacted.

10.3 Evaluating Fit

Understanding consumers' fit preferences could help provide and meet the demand for comfortable, well-fitted clothing for women. It is very important to develop a correlate body shape and fit preferences of consumers. There are different kinds of size charts. Some are body sizes for specific proportions and shapes. Others are for garments including ease allowances which vary according to the garment style and sort of cloth. A drape of the material is its ability to hold out freely in graceful folds when some area of it is supported over a surface and the rest is unsupported (Raj Sharma et al., 2005). Thompson and Anyakoha (2017) emphasized that workers in this industrial sub-sector have a desire for corporate identity, which suggests that clothing should be practical and in line with user requirements. These garments' utility is measured by factors including comfort, safety, ease of movement and activity, aesthetics, and fit. The looks and appearance of the clothed body are the perceptions of the viewer in exceedingly social and environmental status.

Both the available technology for gathering anthropometric data and those for measuring anthropometric attributes are varied. These latter are frequently collected in a variety of forms, including one-dimensional (vector data), two-dimensional (silhouette), and three-dimensional (animation). Height, length, and perimeter of body segments are all included in 1D data, While 2D data includes outlines made of curves or points, silhouettes, or body portions (x, y). The body surface is represented by cloud points with the coordinates (x, y, z) in 3D anthropometry. Traditionally, anthropometric measurements have been made manually with the use of calipers, measuring tapes, and anthropometric metrics. Anthropometric data collection has altered since the advent of 3D technologies. Different technologies exist now for digitizing the 3D representation of the human skeleton. Their primary objective is to produce a 3D digital body model, notwithstanding their disparities. It is possible to create 3D point clouds that depict the 3D body surface by permitting the collection of anthropometric data in various locations. Previous research has demonstrated the importance of the 3D scanning technique for gathering anthropometric information from various human body sections. There is a sizable and widely dispersed number of 3D scanners on the market. They are designed for various body areas, including head, foot, and whole-body scans.

There are four primary categories of technology used for digital measurements of the human body: laser scanning, white light scanning, passive techniques, and technologies based on other active sensors. The 3D software for supply and fit testing remains within the experimental stage. The software can handle standard-type clothes with basic characteristics; the treatment of the asymmetric form remains problematic. The available literature focuses on the "promise" of the technology rather than the techniques and procedures. From the available research, it is evident that the technology is still under development, leading to currently limited functionality. Enabling technologies like CAD/CAM should continue to make it easier to fulfill the individual customer demands by personalizing garments.

Fashion firms face a huge loss of potential as a result of the stark contrast between the shifting consumer requirements, which are less tolerant of conventional items and more demanding of garments with a personalized design, fit, and color/print. The fashion industry would need to switch from a mass-manufacturing business strategy to a mass-customization business model to address this difficulty. Operations involving mass customization might benefit from supply chain management that is optimized for a variety of items. These days, the 1D body's measurements are used as the basis for model creation and categorization for additional

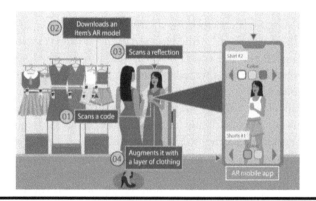

Figure 10.3   Depicting AR on mobile app.

Source: Adapted from **www.scncoft.com**

Figure 10.4   Depicting process of AR scans.

Source: Adapted from **www.scncoft.com**

sizes. The assessment is never algometric, just proportional or logical (taking into consideration the proportions of the body). Poor fit occurs if the specific morphology of the target is not taken into account. With the use of 3D body scanning technology, you may get exact body measurements and a visual representation. The outcomes might be utilized to customize apparel items. The 3D fashion technology of today has outperformed expectations, improving usability and learning curve while perfectly adjusting to the particular apparel design. It is more important than ever to provide the right design on schedule, with the proper fit for the market. As it is today, making fitting clothing might be a major problem for the clothing production sector. Due to their non-standard clothing body sizes, an increasing number of people struggle with clothing sizes. Automated 3D body scanners as shown in Figures 10.2 and 10.3 can now quickly and accurately build a full-scale 3D body model of a person's body by measuring its shape and size. As several authors have demonstrated, this technique aids in the resolution of fit issues by producing precise anthropometric data from 3D body scans.

Customers will be pleased and the industry's environmental effect will be lessened, according to Lisa Bertagnoli's essay from the year 2022. AI applications enable both customers and manufacturers determine the best match situation. According to Carlanda McKinney, founder and CEO of Bodify, the most common reason for returning online-purchased clothing is that it doesn't fit, and returns may cost a merchant up to 38% of the initial purchase price. Customers are asked to provide photographs, and it uses computer vision to determine the size of those images. Machine learning is used to map measurements to the company's stored data. Customers will finally be presented with a range of brands that fit them in the size they personally feel they should be. "Bodyfit data will let producers cut items to sizes that truly fit individuals, coordinate sizes of different types of garments."

Fit for Everybody, a company situated in Princeton, New Jersey, provides consumers with a video that teaches how to measure oneself accurately. Designers, who are Fit for Everybody's paying clients, utilize the data to modify patterns so that they better fit consumers' dimensions. Manufacturers will be able to grade more consistently, or size up and down from the fit model size, with the use of the Fit for Everybody data.

With the use of AI-powered virtual styling tools that guide consumers in selecting things for their body shape, skin tone, and clothing demands, retailers can assist customers in finding the answer to that issue. Online consumers may better understand how a garment will look on them by using AI-driven augmented and virtual reality (AR and VR) capabilities with certain apps, users may project clothes onto their own bodies and then experiment with color, texture, and accessories to find the perfect appearance.

10.4 Effects of AI on the Business World

The digitization of the garment industry and the emergence of the virtual world have advanced, thanks to COVID-19. The crisis not only drove the fashion sectors to inexorably intercommunicate into digital and virtual fashion, but also gave opportunity to reinvent business models toward a lot of sustainable and digital innovation, since COVID-19 had closed down numerous nations globally and barred physical communication between designers and producers. Matthew Drinkwater, head of the Fashion Innovation Agency (FIA), noted that COVID-19 is forcing brands to interact and experiment with immersive technologies (Silva and Bonetti, 2021). Under COVID-19, in particular, the significance of 3D virtual clothing simulations became apparent. They illustrate that COVID-19 has increased corporate interest in the system and that the need for online platform consultation has benefited the system. McQuillan (2020) argued that the benefits of a 3D software system to enhance the garment style method are clear, and this is often significantly evident for zero-waste fashion design.

Technology has supposedly made life easier and more pleasant, according to S. Manisha's comment in the blog *Analytics Steps* (2021). Smart textiles and smart clothing are created in response to the demand for products like fitness trackers and wearable technologies. The rising demand for high-quality products has led to the textile industry's adoption of automation and artificial intelligence (AI) to lower labor and manufacturing costs and produce goods in accordance with client needs. AI makes its mark on every aspect of manufacturing, including prices, textile fabrication, quality assurance, just-in-time delivery, data collection, and computer-integrated manufacturing. Fault detection, pattern verification, and color matching for textile production are other examples of AI applications that are frequently incorporated. In the textile industry, model cutting and design creation are crucial processes in which materials are cut to the required design and various patterns are created on the fabric. Designers may develop and digitize the fundamental elements of patterns using computer-aided design (CAD), a subset of artificial intelligence that makes it possible to produce digital patterns. Patterns are cut using CAD, which allows for the simpler exhibition of concepts and 3D images of the clothing.

According to a recent survey by IMRG Hive, three quarters of fashion shops will invest in AI over the next 24 months, according to the blog *Bloomreach* (2021). Furthermore, there are no indications that this trend will change. Across industries, from big-box shops to direct-to-consumer businesses, artificial intelligence is gaining prominence.

According to an article in a technology journal published in 2022, AI is also poised to excel in the field of sustainable and customized manufacturing. Making 3D representations of one's body as shown earlier in Figure 10.4 is now possible with advances in imaging technology, which makes it easier and less expensive to manufacture personalized apparel. Additionally, workflow and labor management have benefited greatly from artificial intelligence.

DeRoulet (1993) defined mass customization as a possible answer to satisfy customers' wants more accurately while maintaining economies of scale by combining the most effective components of mass production and customization. As a core part of the offerings of mass customizers, Wu (2010) declared that co-design is the method of involving shoppers in co-creating a product, which mixes individual consumers' specifications with a company's predesigned modules, and Fiore et al. (2001) outlined apparel co-design as the process that a client follows to decide a personalized combination of product style, fabric, color, and size from a finite cluster of options. Customization and co-design are recently on the rise in many brands, like Adidas and Nike, as consumers have become more and more demanding, time-driven, information-intensive, and extremely individualistic (Sisodia et al., 2003).

Figure 10.5 Examples of human–AI-collaborated design.

Source: Adapted from Textile Learner

Ulrich et al. (2003) noted that advanced technologies, such as body scanning, CAD, and intelligent systems, empower customers to participate in the style of their merchandise and acquire a fascinating fit; 3D virtual simulation systems can greatly enhance the practicableness of client interaction and customization, meeting dynamic customers' needs (Figure 10.5).

10.5 Utilization of a 3D Virtual Simulation Technology in the Online Clothing Sector

Since the mid-1990s, software platforms and digital media that may be utilized with fashion apparel have led to additional improvements in high fashion, entertainment-related animated apparel, and even commercial goods. Because the use of imaging software like Photoshop, Adobe Illustrator, and After Effects have been common in varied sectors with the influence of the Internet, 2D, 3D, or 4D digital tools have also enabled the forms and motions of garments, and their surfaces and textures to present new digital aesthetics (Clarke and Harris, 2012). Because customers are spending more time online and because online purchasing has been successfully competing with physical marketplaces, the fashion industry still has room to grow. Since the invention of 3D graphics, 3D virtual simulation systems have continuously developed, and they presently allow these modifications. Optitex's 3D Suite, Lectra's Modaris 3D, Assyst Human Solutions Group's Vidya, Techno A's i-Designer, CLO Virtual Fashion's CLO 3D and Marvelous Designer, and Physan's DC Suite are some of the 3D virtual fashion CAD systems available right now. Not only can 3D virtual vesture systems see the interaction between 3D simulations and 2D pattern creations of virtual clothing in real time, but they may also embody complex materials that resemble genuine clothes. By pre-fitting samples of various virtual outfits, 3D simulation systems substantially shorten the duration and cost of the creation process. Similar real-time technologies are used by virtual fitting mirrors in stores and virtual fitting rooms on e-commerce platforms. In comparison to other 3D virtual simulation systems, CLO 3D is now spreading quite quickly in both fashion companies and academic institutions (CLO Virtual Fashion, n.d.; Ju and Jeong, 2016).

10.6 Modern Developments in the Digital Garment Industry

In the fall of 2020, Tommy Hilfiger debuted a line of merchandise modeled by virtual avatars and produced and designed utilizing 3D technology. Virtual showroom avatars were displayed by Balmain by fusing VR (virtual reality) technology with fashion narrative, while Undercover by Jun Takahashi provided a lookbook of 3D-rendered images for the S/S 2021 collection. SUNNEI Canvas, a brand, debuted a new area at the 2021 Digital Fashion Week that, using advanced customizing technology and 3D engineering, combines the actual world with the virtual one. The company displayed a genuine example of dynamic fashion in which animated avatars' attributes, such as forms, fits, and materials, may be changed digitally while they are on screen, modifying how clothing and accessories seem in accordance with the preferences of the viewers. Digital aesthetics have sparked entirely new design concepts and visual expressions as CAD graphic tools and digital technologies have grown more affordable for fashion and textile designers. 3D virtual simulation systems like CLO 3D and Marvelous Designer of CLO Virtual Fashion and DC Suite of Digital Clothing Center are utilized by fashion and game designers alike, and plenty of industrial solutions for garment product development, including Browzwear V-Stitcher, Optitex PDS, and Lectra Modaris 3D now feature 3D visualization furthermore as digital pattern construction (Makryniotis, 2018).

In this manner, 3D dynamic fashion garments can be produced utilizing certain CAD programs by encoding digitally based style, color, and pattern data with computational hardware to demonstrate custom-built designs and diverse transmutable colors and graphics in fashion design. Virtual garment trials are the next big thing that may meld fashion and technology. Globally, computer scientists are aiming to test deep-learning methods that can be used to visually outfit a 3D avatar (digital versions of humans). The Republic of India is also making advancements in this area. A deep learning method known as deep monger developed by two researchers at TCS Research India may be able to forecast how apparel goods would conform to the contours of a person's body.

Although this technology is not new, experts contend that the new method is more accurate. As a result, it enables a person to have a better knowledge of how a piece of clothing will seem on their body. The International Conference on Computer Vision (ICCV) Workshop awarded this technique in 2021. According to TechXplore, "Deep draper is a deep learning-based garment draping system that allows clients to virtually sample garments from a digital closet onto their bodies in 3D." After estimating the client's 3D body form, stance, and body measurements from a photograph or a brief video, the virtual draping is complete. It obtains details about clothing from a seller's digital closet. A neural network is fed the customer's physical measurements by the technology, which then forecasts how the item will appear on the person's 3D avatar.

10.7 Conclusion

Digital attire has the ability to forge a strong connection between the worlds of electronic entertainment and fashion, each of which combines three components of identity, portrayal, and economy to some degree. Digital clothing in particular makes it possible to experiment with fashion trends and even clients' body pictures while inhabiting avatars in social networking sites. Furthermore, the emergence of the Internet has made the way for the area that's not solely virtual in terms of its intangibility but also at the same time discursive in terms of "cybernetic space" (Mitra, 2003, p. 4). Artificial intelligence (AI) "assistance" algorithms can evolve and become much more accurate with a lot of rigorous human-led training. With the insights they generate, brands can make smarter strategic decisions in new business ventures and product development. Real-time clothing simulation using 3D design systems like CLO makes it easy to change styles on the fly. They allow companies to modify styles up to production using real-time AI analysis. In the next fashionable era of personalization and prediction based on customer preferences, the convergence of artificial intelligence, 3D scanning, augmented reality, and computer-generated photography begins.

As digital technology grows more pervasive and personal in our daily lives, the sociocultural traits of fashion as an everyday lifestyle-driven product category are considered online, which might have a long-term impact on the garment business and fashion style development. The advancements in 3D fashion technology have surpassed expectations, making it simpler to use, understand, and adapt to the details of garment design. Today more than ever, it is essential to get the correct design with the proper fit to the market on time. Nowadays, making fitted clothes may well be a vital issue for the garment-producing industry. More and more individuals have trouble with clothing size because of their non-standard clothing body sizes. With advancements in technology, automated 3D body scanners will capture the shape and size of a person's body in seconds and further produce its full-scale 3D body model. AI will concentrate mostly on optimization and speed. Designers may now develop designs more rapidly and economically because of AI's accelerated speed and efficiency. AI's biggest strength will be how quickly it can analyze vast amounts of data and offer design suggestions. Following that, a designer can choose and approve modifications based on that data. The quickest designs to test may be produced, and people can be used to A/B test different prototype versions.

References

Ancutiene, K. (2014). Comparative analysis of real and virtual garment fit. *Industria Textila*, *65*(3), 158–165.

Apeagyei, P. R. (2010). Application of 3D body scanning technology to human measurement for clothing fit. *International Journal of Digital Content Technology and Its Applications*, *4*(7), 58–68.

Berzowska, J., & Coelho, M. (2005, October). Kukkia and vilkas: Kinetic electronic garments. In *Ninth IEEE International Symposium on Wearable Computers (ISWC'05)* (pp. 82–85). IEEE.

Clarke, S. E. B., & Harris, J. (2012). *Digital visions for fashion and textiles: Made in code.* London: Thames and Hudson Ltd.

D'Apuzzo, N. (2007, January). 3D body scanning technology for fashion and apparel industry. In *Videometrics IX* (Vol. 6491, pp. 203–214). SPIE.

Delamore, P., & Sweeney, D. (2010). Everything in 3D: Developing the fashion digital studio. International Conference on 3D Body Scanning Technologies, Lugano, Switzerland, 19–20 October 2010.

DeRoulet, D. G. (1993). Designing—and sustaining the gains from—a service strategy. *Journal of Business Strategy, 14*(1), 21–30.

Devendorf, L., Lo, J., Howell, N., Lee, J. L., Gong, N. W., Karagozler, M. E., . . . & Ryokai, K. (2016, May). "I don't want to wear a screen" probing perceptions of and possibilities for dynamic displays on clothing. In *Proceedings of the 2016 CHI Conference on Human Factors in Computing Systems* (pp. 6028–6039).

Easters, D. J. (2012). Global communication Part 1: The use of apparel CAD technology. *International Journal of Fashion Design, Technology and Education, 5*(1), 45–54.

Fiore, A. M., Lee, S. E., Kunz, G., & Campbell, J. R. (2001). Relationships between optimum stimulation level and willingness to use mass customisation options. *Journal of Fashion Marketing and Management: An International Journal, 5*(2), 99–107.

Geršak, J. (2002). Development of the system for qualitative prediction of garments appearance quality. *International Journal of Clothing Science and Technology, 14*(3/4), 169–180.

Ju, K., & Jeong, Y. (2016). Usage and education of the CLO 3D virtual clothing program in the development office & academic. *Fashion Information and Technology, 13*, 51–59.

Kim, D. E., & LaBat, K. (2013). Consumer experience in using 3D virtual garment simulation technology. *Journal of the Textile Institute, 104*(8), 819–829.

Koo, H. S., Dunne, L., & Bye, E. (2014). Design functions in transformable garments for sustainability. *International Journal of Fashion Design, Technology and Education, 7*(1), 10–20.

Lim, H., & Istook, C. L. (2011). Drape simulation of three-dimensional virtual garment enabling fabric properties. *Fibers and Polymers, 12*, 1077–1082.

Mackey, A., Wakkary, R., Wensveen, S., Hupfeld, A., & Tomico, O. (2019, June). Satisfying a conversation with materials for dynamic fabrics. In *Proceedings of the 2019 on Designing Interactive Systems Conference* (pp. 1047–1058).

Mackey, A., Wakkary, R., Wensveen, S., & Tomico, O. (2017a). "Can I wear this?": Blending clothing and digital expression by wearing dynamic fabric. *International Journal of Design, 11*(3), 51–65.

Mackey, A., Wakkary, R., Wensveen, S., Tomico, O., & Hengeveld, B. (2017b, March). Day-to-day speculation: Designing and wearing dynamic fabric. In *Proceedings of the conference on research through design* (pp. 439–454).

McQuillan, H. (2020). Digital 3D design as a tool for augmenting zero-waste fashion design practice. *International Journal of Fashion Design, Technology and Education, 13*(1), 89–100.

Orth, M. (2004). International fashion machines. http://www.ifmachines.com/. Retrieved September, 20, 2010.

Porterfield, A., & Lamar, T. A. (2017). Examining the effectiveness of virtual fitting with 3D garment simulation. *International Journal of Fashion Design, Technology and Education, 10*(3), 320–330.

Quinn, B. (2012). *Fashion futures*. New York: Merrell.

Raj Sharma, K., Behera, B. K., Roedel, H., & Schenk, A. (2005). Effect of sewing and fusing of interlining on drape behaviour of suiting fabrics. *International Journal of Clothing Science and Technology, 17*(2), 75–90.

Robertson, P. L., Jacobson, D., & Langlois, R. N. (2008). Innovation processes and industrial districts. DCU Business School. RESEARCH PAPER SERIES. PAPER NO. 44. ISSN 1393-290X.

Ross, F. (2009). Iris segmentation using geodesic active contours. *IEEE Transactions on Information Forensics and Security, 4*(4), 824–836.

Ross, F. (2012). A study of how small and medium-sized enterprise tailors utilize e-commerce, social media, and new 3D technological practices. *Fashion Practice, 4*(2), 197–219.

Siersema, I. (2015). The influence of 3D simulation technology on the fashion design process and the consequences for higher education. In *Proceedings of Digital Fashion Conference* (pp. 9–17).

Silva, E. S., & Bonetti, F. (2021). Digital humans in fashion: Will consumers interact? *Journal of Retailing and Consumer Services, 60*, 102430.

Sisodia, R., Wolfe, D., & Sheth, J. N. (2003). *Firms of endearment: How world-class companies profit from passion and purpose.* Hoboken, NJ: Pearson Prentice Hall.

Tao, X., Chen, X., Zeng, X., & Koehl, L. (2018). A customized garment collaborative design process by using virtual reality and sensory evaluation on garment fit. *Computers & Industrial Engineering, 115*, 683–695.

Thompson, D., & Anyakoha, E. (2017). Fit evaluation of functional apparel product developed for female cosmetologists in Lagos, Nigeria. *International Journal of Home Economics, 10*(2), 204–214.

Ulrich, P. V., Jo Anderson-Connell, L., & Wu, W. (2003). Consumer co-design of apparel for mass customization. *Journal of Fashion Marketing and Management: An International Journal, 7*(4), 398–412.

Worbin, L. (2010). In the making: Designing with smart textiles. *Nordic Textile Journal, 2*, 14–19.

Wu, J. (2010). Co-design communities online: Turning public creativity into wearable and sellable fashions. *Fashion Practice, 2*(1), 85–104.

Yu, W., Fan, J. T., & Qian, X. M. (2004). A soft mannequin for the evaluation of pressure garments on human body. *Sen'i Gakkaishi, 60*(2), 57–64.

Chapter 11

Mobile Application and Communication

Viplesh, Manju Kaushik, and Satendra Kumar

11.1 Introduction

The objectives and effects of mobile applications in the corporate, social, and human domains are discussed in this chapter. One of the most important and recently developed fields in the modern data and correspondence age is the mobile application. This chapter demonstrates the use of mobile applications by individual mobile clients as well as their popularity. The outcomes of mobile business applications are presented here. For the purpose of communicating the influence, numerous factual data on the historical development and current state of mobile applications from various geographical locations have been presented. This chapter also includes some effects of the mobile application on society from a moral perspective.

Advanced cell technology has altered how cell phones are understood. Currently, the telephone serves as a crucial component of daily life and correspondence for people as well as being a specialized tool. There is an endless supply of entertainment available thanks to various applications. Undoubtedly, the mobile terminal will determine the organization's future. Right now, the Android platform is becoming more and more well-known in the hardware business, especially the market for smartphones. There are many applications created as a result of the open source, which makes some improved devices free [1].

People were greatly encouraged to use the Android operating system as a result. Additionally, it offers designers a very useful equipment stage that will assist them in realizing their ideas with less effort. As a result, Android can develop farther. Tasks like listening to music, watching videos, tweeting, and other similar activities

DOI: 10.1201/9781003441601-11

can now be transferred from a computer to a phone as PDAs and the Android platform gain popularity [2].

The majority of the applications that are now accessible are corporate applications with extensive underpinning marketing. In the unlikely event that the client chooses to do away with the underlying promotion, a specific fee must be incurred to do so, and this is not advantageous. Meanwhile, many applications created illegal programs to steal client data and compromise client security as a result of the unjustified competition in the industry. At times, clients will focus closer on the client experience of programming [3].

11.2 Mobile Services

An entirely new option for businesses to better service their customers has been provided via remote and mobile systems management. Using mobile communication devices like PDAs, PCs, and cell phones, mobile services will enable customers to make purchases, access news and data, and pay bills. The mobile government sector is another one with a lot of promise for providing services. By enabling citizens to contact taxpayer-funded organizations via mobile devices, mobile devices can improve the concept of e-government [4].

This part centers on mobile trade, featuring the vital highlights of mobile services, depicting the correspondence advances and talking about the various sorts of mobile services.

11.2.1 Features of Mobile Services

- Mobility—The main advantage of mobile services is mobility. Through Internet-capable mobile devices, users can access any information they require, at any time, regardless of where they are. Mobile services meet the demand for constant data and correspondence at any time. Mobile users may participate in activities such as gathering people or traveling while carrying out exchanges or obtaining info using their Internet-enabled mobile devices.
- Reachability—Through mobile devices, business and government representatives may reach customers and constituents whenever and wherever they are. A client can stay in touch and be reachable at any time, wherever, with a mobile terminal. Additionally, the customer has the option to restrict his or her "reachability" to particular individuals or hours.
- Localization—Knowing where a customer is in reality at any given moment also improves mobile services. Numerous area-based services can be offered if area data is available. The smartphone application, for instance, can quickly notify a client when their friend or partner is nearby using information about the client's location. The client may also use it to locate the nearest restaurant or ATM.

Figure 11.1   Features of mobile services [1].

■ Personalization—Although there are currently tremendous volumes of information, services, and apps available on the Internet, not all data is pertinent to all consumers. Mobile services can be personalized to provide data in ways that are appropriate for a specific user or to channel services in ways that are appropriate for that user [5] (Figure 11.1).

11.3 Government in Motion

The expansion of e-government into mobile is known as mobile government. Through websites on the Internet, people are given the ability to contact government agencies and organizations regardless of their location or the time of day using mobile devices.

The government and its constituents (G2C), business and its citizens (G2B), representatives (G2E), and the government and itself (G2G) could all be associated in a way that is appropriate and extremely valuable. It's anticipated that soon, mobile constituents will genuinely wish to pay their taxes, get birth certificates, renew their licenses, reserve campsites, and access other services via their mobile device. Constituents can now expect more flexibility, responsiveness, and individualized services from their states in the era of mobile government [6].

The development and deployment of supporting technology will determine how quickly mobile services evolve. Network technologies, service technologies, mobile middleware, mobile commerce terminals, mobile location technologies, mobile customization technologies, and content delivery and format are only a few of these technologies. The following are some of the key technologies that are bringing mobile services to life [7]:

■ GSM—The global system for mobile communication, or GSM, is the dominant mobile standard in Europe and the majority of Asia-Pacific. It operates

Figure 11.2 Mobile government [6].

in the 900 MHz and 1800 MHz frequency bands (1900 MHz in the USA). GPRS (general packet radio service) and HSCSD (high-speed circuit switched data) are two more network technologies that are built on top of it. It is economically feasible to create cutting-edge mobile services and applications since the GSM standard has been widely adopted (Figure 11.2).

■ SMS—Text messages can be sent to and received from mobile phones via SMS, or short messaging service. Currently, an SMS message can exchange up to 160 alphanumeric characters. SMS messages, which are widely utilized in Europe, are mostly used for simple one-to-one texting and voice mail notifications. Additionally, it offers on-the-go access to information services like news, stock quotations, sports, and weather. The development and plan of empowering developments will determine how popular SMS chat, which is the newest feature, becomes. These advancements incorporate but are not restricted to network advances, administration innovations, mobile middleware, mobile business terminals, versatile area innovations, mobile personalization advancements, content conveyance, and what's more, design. Introduced in the following are a portion of the significant innovations that are making mobile services a reality [8].

■ Bluetooth—A low-power radio technology for data sharing and communication, Bluetooth is named after a Danish lord who conquered Scandinavia in the tenth century. The Bluetooth short-range remote standard, which supports local networks and uses a single chip with integrated radio transmission circuitry, is a viable one (LANs). It was designed to swap out all of the linkages and infrared connections inside a ten-meter circle. PCs, printers, portable devices, and PDAs can all be used to connect electronic devices to distant information networks via Bluetooth [9].

■ GPS—A network of satellites in orbit around the planet makes up the global positioning system (GPS). GPS receivers can pinpoint the precise geographic area with exceptional accuracy because the satellites are constantly broadcasting their own position and orientation. Originally developed in the USA for military usage, GPS is now also used by average citizens. GPS, for instance, is utilized in automobile navigation systems [10].

■ XML—A meta-language called Extensible Markup Language (XML) was created to convey the significance of information using a self-descriptive system. It tags data and also integrates material into the environment, enabling content providers to incorporate semantics into their publications. As long as the associations agree on the significance of the information that is communicated, information can be traded directly even between affiliations with different activity frameworks and information models for XML consistent data frameworks [11].

11.3.1 Past and Present of Mobile Application

At first, the mobile applications that came with our initial phones were morning alarms, calculator, mini-computers, and so forth. At that time, individuals just utilized mobile applications for getting caller ID, doing straightforward computations, and so on. Be that as it may, the mobile application engineers kept asking, "Why simple?" But they realized that later on, mobile applications would develop extensively and everyone would utilize them. In 2000, the mobile application engineers were talking about web-based mobile applications. With the mobile application, individuals can associate themselves with the web for their everyday needs [4, 12] (Figures 11.3 to 11.7).

There are a few places of the world where mobile business was behind the times, like European Union Association (EUA). In that area of the planet, mobile

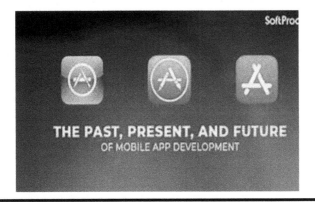

Figure 11.3   The past, present, and future of mobile application [4].

Source: Adapted from https://softprodigy.com/an-insight-into-the-past-present-and-future-of-mobile-app-development/

organizations were not really progressing. Because of this, mobile applications were assumed to be merely entertaining. Yet, if we consider Europe, the world's greatest mobile organization like Nokia, Ericsson, and other emerged from that region with the modern mobile advancement. The fundamental issue is that those organizations were making phones for the mobile administrator likewise they were making the mobile application. In any case, they might slow things down [13, 14].

These created a gap between the client and the engineer. Engineers were dissatisfied with their creations, whether they were designed for a future event or not. Back in America, a long time ago, a company announced that it was developing a mobile phone that would alter consumer behavior. The list of requests made to the administrator couldn't have bothered them less. They had to create a cell phone and mobile application that would be sold, which they ultimately did [15, 16].

The iPhone, when it was delivered, it turned out to be generally needed. Furthermore, other cell organizations are as yet attempting to duplicate it. The principal element of this PDA was that it had an incredible phase that permitted running very dynamic applications. They have sold countless such applications [17].

Nokia also launched its application store. For instance, Nokia uses the Symbian operating system, and the "Ovi Store" is a sizable app store where we can discover numerous tools for our daily necessities. It is also a fantastic location for designers. Sony Ericsson also offers Android OS and Android Market [18].

The majority of applications rely on the Internet and offer fantastic elements. After that, mobile web usage significantly increases. These mobile applications are made to assist us in our daily lives and provide us the ability to connect to the Internet, communicate with other people, gather information from far-off locations, engage in social correspondence using Facebook or Twitter, locate specific places, and more. You're on your way home so you can use your phone to cool the inside air before you get there. Additionally, you can wirelessly receive alerts for your house or car, among other things [19, 20].

In 2008, there was an interesting achievement: the number of mobile broadband customers surpassed the number of fixed broadband customers. However, mobile web access still experiences issues with both ease of use and interoperability [21].

11.3.2 Mobiles in Business

All of the cell phones and component telephones have a savvy climate and a tremendous number of mobile applications. A large portion of the applications interface individuals to the world by means of Internet or mobile broadband. For instance, Google supports maps, routes, email, entertainment, gaming, and e-commerce. So, overall, mobile clients use the web via mobile applications and mobile administrators. Furthermore, other outsider organizations carry on with work by giving broadband network access [22].

Figure 11.4   Use of mobile in business [2].

Source: Adapted from https://martech.org/think-smartphones-just-bottom-funnel-think/

In the most recent couple of years, the use of mobile broadband has increased significantly all around the world; however, not all over. According to a research study, the regions with the highest numbers of mobile broadband subscribers include Asia, the Pacific, and Europe [23, 24].

11.3.3 Market of Mobile Applications

The different mobile working frameworks have been given by the different mobile organizations. Also, most mobile organizations have their own mobile application market: iPhone application market, BlackBerry application market, Android market, and so on [25, 26].

From those web-based markets, mobile clients can download numerous valuable mobile applications. Some applications are free or furnished by an organization with a handset, and some applications the client needs to pay for in order to download [27, 28].

Consistently countless mobile applications are downloaded by mobile clients. So this is a major business area. There are numerous highly profitable mobile producer businesses as well as business managers or mobile application engineer organizations. The mobile web is also being used by the phone client to download that product. Not only does the client download the mobile application, but they can also download games, music, and other entertainment content. As indicated by a study by the mobile application store administrator GetJar, by 2012, the market for mobile applications will be worth $17.5 billion. When that time comes, the number of mobile application downloads will also have increased to about 50 billion from just over 7 billion in 2009 [29].

Figure 11.5 Mobile applications market [26].

In any case, as GetJar organizer and CEO Ilja Laurs made the strong expectation that "mobile applications will obscure the customary work area Internet," even venturing to such an extreme as to say that "cell phones will kill the work area [30]."

11.4 Mobile Device Use for Education

Students, instructors, content, climate, and an appraisal are basic parts of mobile learning. The most significant elements of mobile learning are movability, portability, availability, adaptability, intuitiveness, setting responsiveness, distinction, and openness. Mobile learning is famous in the age of e-learning. As a result of new cell phones with upgraded abilities, for example, high-power cameras, huge capacity limits, enormous screen sizes, longer battery duration, top-notch voice processing, etc., the interest level of language teachers (especially English teachers) has expanded [22].

Mobile applications increase motivation, make the growing experience more interesting and enjoyable, and assist with working on the abilities of the students in a positive way. Involving cell phones in learning English as a second language acquired positive criticism from both educators and learners, gives seriously fascinating learning environments, and permits cooperative activities, prompt criticism to students, close connection for students, and increment learning performance [25].

11.4.1 Learning English in Mobile Application

The most troublesome ability for new students of the English language is pronunciation. Some of the researchers have revealed that the expertise of elocution has gotten a great deal of interest since it is a striking element of any language. Many research studies done in the past demonstrate that the right articulation is vital to communicating yourself to others intelligibly. In this manner, it is evident that it is expected to

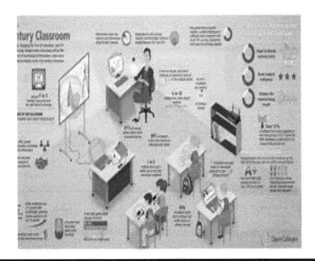

Figure 11.6   Use of mobile device in education [22].

complete more examinations on learning and showing the right elocution skills. It is clear that any individual with mistaken articulation can't communicate themselves accurately and effectively and there is the additional gamble that they may not be understood by others. Poor elocution means poor communication ability. So, it is essential to learn the right articulation even though it is complicated and difficult. The utilization of the discourse acknowledgment innovation in showing a language subject to new students is an exceptionally new concept and it very well may be found in the literature that more studies are being completed in this field [31, 32].

11.4.2 Intelligent Systems

An intelligent schooling system is such a framework that can adjust to the learning climate by evolving the training techniques to best suit the students' capacities. Intelligent systems assume a significant part in schooling since such frameworks show the students at the right level with the goal that the students benefit the most from the framework and additionally become spurred during the learning process. Every person has a varied learning capacity and rate of learning. In the clever framework created by the creator, the levels of the students have been evaluated prior to the start of the learning, and afterward, the education goes on at the level generally appropriate to the students [19].

Thus, the inspiration of the self-students is not disturbed and the learning happens with pleasure. In such cases where the level is too hard for the student, then the person might feel inspired, become motivated, and have free trust in learning the new material [14].

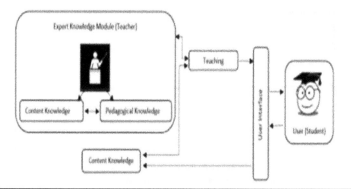

Figure 11.7   Developed intelligent adaptive teaching system [32].

Source: Adapted from www.google.com/imgres?imgurl=https%3A%2F%2Fmedia. springernature.com%2Flw685%2Fspringer-static%2Fimage%2Fart%253A10. 1007%252Fs10639-020-10182-8%2FMediaObjects%2F10639_2020_10182_ Fig1_HTML.png&imgrefurl=https%3A%2F%2Flink.springer.com%2 Farticle%2F10.1007%2Fs10639-020-10182-8&tbnid=DeP5OKH5-uGuwM&ve t=12ahUKEwit2IWI04r9AhUBz3MBHeCoCL8QMygDegQIARBJ..i&docid=DR CAwhJEdMXqUM&w=685&h=239&q=Fig.7%20Developed%20intelligent%20 adaptive%20teaching%20system%20&hl=hi&ved=2ahUKEwit2IWI04r9AhUBz 3MBHeCoCL8QMygDegQIARBJ

11.5 Mobile Application's Effect in Society

The mobile application has a remarkable impact on the public as well as individuals and enterprises. Mobile applications can help the entire society function. A few social impact issues are shown here [17].

Fast correspondence: Numerous mobile applications, including Facebook, Twitter, Courier, Skype, and Google Talk, facilitate communication between members of the general public. Where the topographical distance is not a factor, they can still communicate. As a result, the social bond strengthens. This is also fantastic for family, friends, and society.

Save time and increase efficiency: In the public arena or in countries individuals can do their day-to-day work like browse email and contact business associates at any time in transport, whether the train, vehicle, or walking, so there is no need to stand by in a room or office. This also saves time and provides individuals additional opportunities to work. The efficiency of a society's or nation's workforce is expanding progressively and it is very important to develop IT framework in the emerging nations. In emerging nations, the purposes of mobile applications work on the information on individuals. Subsequently, the IT foundation works in any emerging nation [22].

Increase job opportunity: More jobs are becoming available in the public sector due to the development of mobile applications and the mobile application industry. There are so many jobs available in this field. This is very significant for a society or nation.

Less power utilization by PCs: When a significant part of the people use mobile applications for their routine, performing everyday tasks and accessing offices via mobile applications, PC usage and power consumption will decrease.

Impressive cost saving: People can use a mobile voice over Internet protocol (VoIP) application to make international calls from their mobile device. As a result, monthly consumption drops.

Entertainment: Utilizing mobile applications, individuals in the public arena can entertain themselves [27].

11.6 Conclusion and Future Scope

There are many technologies in our evolving world that have great potential for mobile app development, including AI and ML, IoT and cloud, 5G technology, blockchain, AR and VR, wearables, cross-platform apps, and Swift. Real-time conversation translation is a goal that can be accomplished with the aid of AI in mobile app development. You can learn more about user behavior by using the smarter apps. Mobile app development will reach entirely new heights as a result of the AI in mobile applications, which is revolutionizing technology. Future applications must be more sophisticated. They will need to connect with you in the same manner that IoT-based gadgets do. The capacity of the cloud to connect several devices with APIs will be crucial in the creation of mobile applications in the future.

References

[1] Valerie Christopherson. Mobile Marketing Association, 2008, https://www.mmaglobal.com/news/mobile-marketing-association-announces-2008-event-line.

[2] Bin Yang, Yang-Yang Hao, Jie Wang, Zhi-Hua Hu "Flexible service architecture for maritime business promotion based on mobile technology," 2010. IEEE. DOI: 10.1109/NSWCTC.2010.269.

[3] E.W.T. Ngai, A. Gunasekaran, "A review for mobile commerce research and applications", Decision Support Systems 2007; 43(1): 3–15.

[4] Mobile applications—past, present and future, Posted by Diogo Caldeira Pires, July 2, 2009, http://mobilemondayportugal.com/?p=180.

[5] International Telecommunications Union, "The World in 2009: ICT facts and figures", 2009.

[6] Mobile Web, "Wikipedia", http://en.wikipedia.org/wiki/Mobile_Web.

[7] The Nielsen Company, "The state of mobile apps", September 2010, https://www.nielsen.com/insights/2010/the-state-of-mobile-apps-2/.

[8] K. Siau, E. Lim, Z. Shen, "Mobile commerce: promises, challenges and research agenda", Journal of Database Management 2001; 12(3): 3–10.

[9] Bluetooth White Paper, "The official bluetooth websites", www.bluetooth.com/developer/whitepaper/whitepaper.asp

[10] F. Muller-Veerse, "Mobile commerce report", *Durlacher Corporation*, 2000. www.durlacher.com/downloads/mcomreport.pdf

[11] N. Adriana, "Uses of mobile applications for smart phones", http://ezinearticles.com/?Uses-OfMobile-Applications-For-SmartPhones&id=5161301 (accessed 24 October 2022).

[12] S. Kumar, M. Mittal, V. K. Yadav, "Cost-effective product prioritisation technique for software product line testing," International Journal of Engineering Systems Modelling and Simulation 2021; 12(2–3): 83–93.

[13] Eric Slivka, "Flurry: 22% of recent mobile applications starts targeting iPad", April 2, 2010, www.macrumors.com/2010/04/02/flurry-22

[14] Anuj Khanna, The future of mobile application storefronts, Wireless Expertise Ltd, 2009.

[15] C. Huang, P. Sun, "Using mobile technologies to support mobile multimedia English listening exercises in daily life", 2010, http://nhcuer.lib.nhcue.edu.tw/ir/bitstream/392440000Q/649/1/120.pdf (accessed 1 June 2016).

[16] R. Godwin-Jones, "Emerging technologies mobile apps for language learning", Language Learning and Technology 2011; 15(2): 2–11.

[17] C. S. J. Huang, S. J. H. Yang, T. H. C. Chiang, A. Y. S. Su, "Effects of situated mobile learning approach on learning motivation and performance of EFL students", Educational Technology & Society 2016; 19(1): 263–276.

[18] H.-Y. Hsu, S.-K. Wang, L. Comac, "Using audioblogs to assist English-language learning: an investigation into student perception", Computer Assisted Language Learning 2008; 21(2): 181–198.

[19] C.-M. Chen, S.-H. Hsu, "Personalized intelligent mobile learning system for supportive effective English learning", Educational Technology and Society Journal 2008; 11(3): 153–180.

[20] N. Cavus, D. Ibrahim, "Learning English using children's stories in mobile device", British Journal of Educational Technology 2016, http://onlinelibrary.wiley.com/doi/10.1111/bjet.12427/abstract (accessed 27 May 2016).

[21] A. Ambegaonkar, C. Ritchie, S. de la Fuente Garcia, "The use of mobile applications as communication aids for people with dementia: Opportunities and limitations", Journal of Alzheimer's Disease Reports 2021; 5(1): 681–692.

[22] J. Jia, Y. Chen, Z. Ding, M. Ruan, "Effects of a vocabulary acquisition and assessment system on students' performance in a blended learning class for English subject", Computers & Education 2012; 58(1): 63–76.

[23] G. M. Chinnery, "Emerging technologies, going to the mall: mobile assisted language learning", Language Learning and Technology Journal 2006; 10(1). http://llt.msu.edu/vol10num1/emerging/default.html (accessed 12 May 2016).

[24] S. Kumar; R. Kumar, M. Mittal, "A hybrid approach to perform test case prioritisation and reduction for software product line testing", International Journal of Vehicle Autonomous Systems 2020; 15(3/4).

[25] J. Yang, "Mobile assisted language learning: review of the recent applications of emerging mobile technologies", Canadian Center of Science and Education Journal 2013; 6(7). www.ccsenet.org/journal/index.php/elt/article/view/28000/0 (accessed 31 May 2016).

[26] "Global Mobile Application Market (2010–2015) Markets and Markets", August 2010, www.researchandmarkets.com/research/9692 cd/global_mobile_appl.

[27] I.-J. Chen, C.-C. Chang, J.-C. Yen, "Effects of presentation mode on mobile language learning: a performance efficiency perspective", Australasian Journal of Educational Technology 2012; 28(1): 122–137.

[28] M. J. Munro, T. M. Derwing, "A prospectus for pronunciation research in the 21st century: a point of view", Journal of Second Language Pronunciation 2015; 1(1): 11–42.

[29] Anand Srinivasan, "Fastest growing mobile app categories", 17 June 2010, http://gorumors.com/crunchies/fastest-growingmobile-app-categories/.

[30] Nick O'Neill, "Facebook has over 4 million daily mobile users", 2 February 2009, www.allfacebook.com/facebookdaily-mobile-users-2009-02.

[31] M. Hillebrand, "Amazon and sprint expand wireless shopping", 2000, www.ecommercetimes.com/perl/story/2600.html

[32] S. K. Pangeni, "Use of mobile application for communication, interaction and learning: Lessons from an action research", Journal of Training and Development 2021; 6(1): 60–70.

Chapter 12

Emerging and Growing Technologies in Blockchain Security
A Review

Vidit Kesarwani, Honey Gocher, Amit K Singh, and Yudhveer Singh

12.1 Introduction

Blockchain is a type of chain structure which binds multiple data blocks in a synchronized manner, assuring that such a distributed ledger cannot be amended or cryptographically fabricated. The distributed ledger makes it different because it works differently from the traditional network. In the traditional network structure, the power usually resides with the central authority that is assigned, and all the decisions are made under the central authority. In case of a distributed ledger, the controls are distributed by multiple rules and there is no central authority for the control. Blockchain can tolerate erratic patterns attributing to the peer-to-peer network protocol, retaining the relevant business logic [1, 2]. The technology used in the blockchain has all the capabilities to bring substantial upgrades in various sectors like IoT, financial sector, voting, medical department, insurance, education, etc. Blockchains can mitigate cybersecurity risks and incorporate security features in some specific ways: (i) Blockchain makes the network more resilient by preventing single-point failure. (ii) Blockchain employs a consensus methodology that assures the ledger's integrity and transparency. (iii) It is extremely challenging for hackers or attackers to intrude or use malicious payload or malware [3] (Figure 12.1).

DOI: 10.1201/9781003441601-12

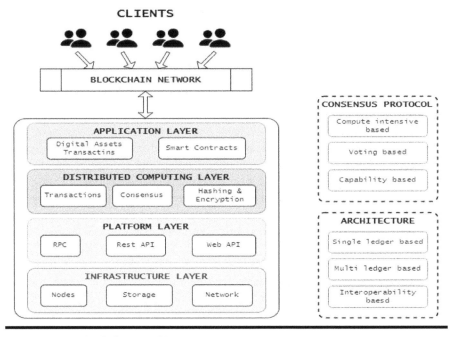

Figure 12.1   Blockchain architecture.

Various evaluations on blockchain security have been undertaken from multiple viewpoints, exposing certain research gaps and suggesting some future avenues for scholars and practitioners to explore. Blockchain's security approach focuses on the use of security technologies and procedures to identify, prevent, and respond to attacks at varying tiers. Joshi et al. [4] evaluated consensus mechanisms in terms of ensuring data security and privacy. But there still exist some security problems with other things, like smart contracts, majority attacks, cost problems, and data scale.

12.2 Categories of Blockchain

Here, it's important to keep in mind that blockchains are safe and secure by design. The difficulty of falsifying information or attempting to modify data would be high along with the expenditure (Figure 12.2). There exist four categories of blockchain technologies.

1) **Public Blockchain:** "For the people, by the people, and of the people" is the main aim of this blockchain. Anyone who has access to the Internet can register for the blockchain platform to become an authentication node. This should likewise imply that the exchange and tracking of cryptocurrency transactions

is by far the most prominent use for public blockchain technology given that the first public blockchain was utilized for digital currency. Notarizing papers and keeping track of public property ownership data are two other possible uses for a public blockchain. The key thing to remember is that any data that has to be both accessible and safe is best achieved by a public blockchain.

2) **Private Blockchain:** Unlike public blockchains, this one has an administrator who oversees crucial functions like read/write access and who all must be granted permission to read. Private blockchains may be used for a diversity of tasks, such as supply chain management, private voting, and safeguarding trade secrets. There are restrictions on who may access the data and add data to the chain in a private blockchain. The data is not accessible to outside parties. Because they have fewer nodes than public blockchains, they often operate more quickly.

3) **Consortium Blockchain:** In a semi-decentralized blockchain, many organizations oversee running a network. Representatives of a known group may only access the blockchain, removing some of the hazards associated with having a centralized authority supervise the network, as would be the scenario with a private blockchain. A consortium blockchain is mostly used in the banking and payments industries. Theoretically, banks might organize a consortium and choose which node would oversee authenticating any transactions. The benefit of developing a consortium blockchain would be that it provides access control similar to a private or hybrid blockchain while being more secure and flexible than a public blockchain.

4) **Hybrid Blockchain:** The private blockchain network infrastructure is used to create the hashed data blocks for the hybrid blockchain. Then, without sacrificing data privacy, the data is stored in a public blockchain. The company has control over who may access and update data to the blockchain. The hybrid blockchain is owned by a private party, but it cannot change transactions. Because it is more challenging to corrupt or control 51% of the nodes, it is more secure than a private blockchain. Any user's identity is masked from other end user until they conduct a transaction, which is another essential feature of a hybrid blockchain. Being one of the most emerging and growing technologies, it comes with some benefits like the following:

1) **Transparency:** It becomes one of the most essential parts of the blockchain technology. When we talk about the basic database systems, they always had restrictions like the datasets being password protected [5]. Unlike them, the blockchain technology allows all the users in the network to see what all changes are made into the database. The changes then done in the database become rigid and these are not altered after that under any condition.

2) **Decentralized System:** Since we know that there is no single authority for any entity in the blockchain technology, the customers are able to have control on the basis of some set of rules [6].

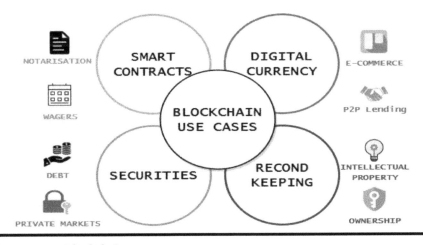

Figure 12.2   Blockchain use cases.

3) **Load Balancing:** The computing of the transactions and the physical assets of the blockchain are spread around the globe, this helps in the load balancing proficiency.
4) **Unlimited Usage Technology:** Blockchain works wherever some kind of data is present in any application. Cryptocurrency is a part of Blockchain technology.
5) **No Third-Party Inclusion:** All the data interchange and transactions in this era are completed through a medium (like Paytm, PayPal, etc.). The blockchain system is based on the methodology whereby all the senders and recipients have individual access to the system and no third-party vendor is involved.

12.3 Process Security in Blockchain

To ensure the security of an organization's network systems, attendees in a business process must choose and follow certain standards. The complexity of blockchain security at the process level is imposed by several duties and governance [7]. The possible four aspects in the security of the process can be briefed as follows.

12.3.1 Smart Contract Security

Without an externally trusted third party, smart contracts are scripts that are pre-configured on a distributed network of nodes that have mutual mistrust for one another [8]. To large datasets transactions between the parties, smart contracts expose transaction history to the risk of disclosing personal information. Else difficulties are faced in the supervision of these contracts and the data. Criminal Smart Contracts (CSC), a brand-new crucial cyberweaponry, may be used by criminals to generate data transactions with zero-day vulnerabilities. One of the biggest causes of cybersecurity threats at the blockchain process level is the smart contract. In addition, once issued, a smart contract is rarely able to be changed [9]. If any kind of malicious data or recorded fault is registered in the blockchain application, then it cannot be removed or changed.

When talking about the smart contracts, we basically look upon three different levels or the layers on which it works. The first is the business level, then we have it on the virtual machine layer, and lastly it comes on the contracts coding level [10]. Unauthorized access, adverse application infection, inconsistent state, and transaction-ordering reliance are examples of business-level security vulnerabilities. Issues with time restrictions, stack size limits, and random number generation are all security concerns at the virtual machine level. The security of smart contracts at the code level is a crucial problem for blockchain applications [11]. It is extremely important to capture the semantics and security features of contracts from the bytecode that is currently being executed to validate their security. SECURIFY, a security analyzer that automatically extracts explicit semantic data about a smart contract's security from the code, has been developed by Tsankov et al. [8]. To automatically build smart contracts by the help of some kind of structural patterns, a semantic approach is required in the meantime of process the designing the contracts [12]. To properly automate the creation of smart contracts on such a blockchain, intricate semantics continue to promote significant challenges.

12.3.2 Implementation Security of Blockchain

In addition to the well-known cryptocurrencies and blockchain-based fintech applications, there are other blockchain implementations in the contexts of the Internet of Things (IoT), artificial intelligence, shared prudence, medical and health insurance databases, modern city, social fabrication, and supply chain management. Thorough testing of vital code is necessary for the implementation of high security.

A critical empowering technology for how devices interact and exchange data to support humans in gaining insights is all about Internet of Things (IoT) [13]. However, the IoT network is exposed to cyber risks and assaults due to a lack of security countermeasures, which has an impact on privacy and safeguarding of the concerned parties.

Through a bi-directional information flow, a smart grid is intended to provide advanced consumption monitoring and energy trading. Blockchain can help to address the reliability issue of decentralized energy exchanges by allowing autonomous and integrable cross negotiations and bargaining based on contracts between decentralized energy providers and clients. Despite the fact that blockchain promises to make it easier for industrial partners to share information, it is crucial for decision-makers to understand their unique circumstances in sight of their individual business settings. Another challenge with the adoption of blockchain-based systems is their scalability.

12.3.3 Operation Standards and Regulations

In terms of scalability, performance, and system compatibility, blockchain is still in its infancy. Businesses confront managerial issues as well as technological ones since inscrutable institutional, administrative, sociological, economic, and technical hardware systems must be integrated with blockchain [14]. With their own standards and codes, open-source blockchain platforms make it difficult to achieve uniform approaches across borders. For blockchain to be successfully implemented, participants must be safeguarded, and system resilience must be improved against cyberattacks [15]. The capability of blockchain to grow is greatly constrained by the absence of universal standards and explicit laws.

But rather than a technological problem, laws and regulations will have a greater impact on the complexity of emerging security risks. It is also viable to assess the effectiveness of blockchains' data processing using a benchmarking mechanism [16]. Standards must be established to solve issues with security, resilience, privacy protection, and administration in blockchain deployments to foster confidence.

12.3.4 Risk Assessment and Fraud Detection

Fraud detection is a critical component of security in the execution of enterprise systems like the system for tax administration. Data mining and classification analysis can be used to find or compress the rules and methods. Researchers used the blockchain to tackle several information system fraud detection difficulties.

12.4 Data Security in Blockchain

Data security in the blockchain may be divided into three categories: availability, confidentiality, and integrity. This study explores blockchain data security challenges from the perspectives of cryptography, signature protocols, encryption methods (including processing and retrieval), privacy safeguards, and consensus algorithms.

12.4.1 Access Control in Blockchain

Access control has become more complicated in evolving information systems from integrated systems to distributed, cloud-based, and blockchain-based applications [5]. Fine-grained access to decentralized data is often maintained in blockchain research [6, 17] by merging smart contract and attribute-based encrypting (ABE) techniques. A smart contract may represent the logical semantics of authorization, maintain the modified ciphertext of ABE, and provide flexible policies for access control for adding and deleting data. After the data has been encrypted, the ABE schema links the private key to a particular set of characteristics.

A potential option to allow network access is a blockchain that may be used to safeguard and regulate access to the data. For the purpose of storing participant data posts in long-term isolated contexts, A multimodal fine-grained access control strategy for blockchain was developed by Adams. Blockchain [17, 18] access control methods are notoriously difficult to use or implement. It is essential in practice to develop an effective and simple approach that allows for both privacy and granular access control on a blockchain.

12.4.2 Privacy Protection Techniques in Blockchain

The supplied data's delicacy or degree of safety are not specified by the blockchain, even though it employs asymmetric encryption [19]. The fundamental objective of blockchain systems' data security level is the protection of user privacy [20]. Hierarchical clustering and correlation analysis on an open decentralized system may still be used to easily extract sensitive data. A user can use the zero-knowledge proof (ZKP) paradigm to strongly suggest to another user that a given assertion is true without disclosing any additional information [11]. Completeness, soundness, and zero-knowledge qualities are satisfied by a zero-knowledge proof. Even when the facts are secret, zero-knowledge proofs can ensure that transactions are accurate.

12.5 Research Aspiration

Blockchain necessitates a technical, administrative, governance analytic, and cyber-security intelligence solution. Future directions are gathered in light of the analysis just mentioned.

12.5.1 Enhancing Process Security in Blockchain

1) **Introducing a Smart Debugging Technique:** Blockchain implementation procedures may present unexpected weaknesses if cryptographic techniques are widely used. One of the biggest obstacles for blockchain is continually doing transactions in a safe manner. To demonstrate the system's inevitable consistency and correctness criteria, an executable semantics model can be created.

2) **Analytics of Big Data for Blockchain:** Since participant behaviors in a block-chain network could be tracked, many blockchains have countermeasures to

Table 12.1 Signature Algorithms and Privacy Protection Methodology in Blockchain Technology

Techniques	Advantages	Security Issues	References
Homomorphic Encryption	Forbidding the decryption key from being used to perform arbitrary computations on the encoded data series	Inadequate execution of homomorphic encryption	[7, 14, 19]
Secure Data Provenance	Maintaining a history of the dataset's creation, modification, and activities	The origins data's accessibility and anonymity	[5, 20, 21]
Multi- Signatures	Numerous keys needed to achieve a transaction	Cyberattack involving original signature forgery	[19, 22, 23]
Group/Ring Signature	The integration of a linked anonymity trait	Secrecy of the data in any postquantum application	[21, 24, 25]
Zero- Knowledge Proof	By exposing the statement's authenticity, the user can persuade the other person that indeed the remark is true.	Poor scalability, massive cost of proof creation, and sophisticated engineering	[4, 26]

preserve user transaction privacy, such as one-time credentials and secret keys, but they are insufficiently reliable to be effective [27]. AI technology would produce more trustworthy results once the veracity of information can be guaranteed on blockchain (Table 12.1).

12.5.2 Enhancing Data Security in Blockchain

1) **Methods for Anti-Quantum Computing Signatures:** The transaction's signature is a critical element of the transactional data records. The classic public-key protocols, including RSA (Rivest, Shamir, Adleman), DSA (Digital Signature Algorithm), and several others, have become obsolete due to the quick advancement of quantum computing research.

2) **Highly Efficient Consensus Algorithms:** To achieve data consistency across all distributed system participants, consensus procedures are essential. In general, earlier research generally used probabilistic analysis based on a synthesis of distributed components to examine the security features of consensus

methods. Finding an efficient collection of attributes, modeling choices, protocol modifications, and constraints in the application of these algorithms are all problems that have yet to be addressed.

12.6 Conclusion

This study explores the current state of blockchain security concerns and outlines areas for future information systems and services research. The process level and the data level are the two categories used to describe the security of the blockchain. Our analysis also looks at how much attention has been given to these security concerns. Promising research avenues for blockchain security are presented based on findings from the study of research concerns. In this period of rapid progress, we think that our study represents important conceptual and technical advancements. We also expect that our work will help establish blockchain security as a new area for operational research and engineering.

Declaration of Interest

The authors declare that they have no known competing financial interests or personal relationships that could have appeared to influence the work reported in this paper.

References

[1] Wang, T., Hua, H., Wei, Z., & Cao, J. (2022). Challenges of blockchain in new generation energy systems and future outlooks. International Journal of Electrical Power & Energy Systems, 135, 107499.

[2] Taylor, P. J., Dargahi, T., Dehghantanha, A., Parizi, R. M., & Choo, K. K. R. (2020). A systematic literature review of blockchain cyber security. Digital Communications and Networks, 6(2), 147–156.

[3] Leng, J., Zhou, M., Zhao, J. L., Huang, Y., & Bian, Y. (2020). Blockchain security: A survey of techniques and research directions. IEEE Transactions on Services Computing, 15(4), 2490–2510.

[4] Joshi, A. P., Han, M., & Wang, Y. (2018). A survey on security and privacy issues of blockchain technology. Mathematical Foundations of Computing, 1(2), 121.

[5] Centobelli, P., Cerchione, R., Del Vecchio, P., Oropallo, E., & Secundo, G. (2022). Blockchain technology for bridging trust, traceability and transparency in circular supply chain. Information & Management, 59(7), 103508.

[6] Hsiao, J. H., Tso, R., Chen, C. M., & Wu, M. E. (2017). Decentralized E-voting systems based on the blockchain technology. In *Advances in computer science and ubiquitous computing* (pp. 305–309). Springer, Singapore.

[7] Mavridou, A., & Laszka, A. (2018, February). Designing secure ethereum smart contracts: A finite state machine-based approach. In *International Conference on Financial Cryptography and Data Security* (pp. 523–540). Springer, Berlin, Heidelberg.

[8] Tsankov, P., Dan, A., Drachsler-Cohen, D., Gervais, A., Buenzli, F., & Vechev, M. (2018, October). Securify: Practical security analysis of smart contracts. In *Proceedings of the 2018 ACM SIGSAC Conference on Computer and Communications Security. ACM, USA* (pp. 67–82).

[9] Bartoletti, M., & Pompianu, L. (2017, April). An empirical analysis of smart contracts: platforms, applications, and design patterns. In *International Conference on Financial Cryptography and Data Security* (pp. 494–509). Springer, Cham.

[10] Ramachandran, A., & Kantarcioglu, D. (2017). Using blockchain and smart contracts for secure data provenance management. arXiv:1709.10000.

[11] Dasgupta, D., Shrein, J. M., & Gupta, K. D. (2019). A survey of blockchain from security perspective. Journal of Banking and Financial Technology, 3(1), 1–17.

[12] Ratta, P., Kaur, A., Sharma, S., Shabaz, M., & Dhiman, G. (2021). Application of blockchain and internet of things in healthcare and medical sector: Applications, challenges, and future perspectives. *Journal of Food Quality*, 2021, 1–20.

[13] Zhou, L., Wang, L., Sun, Y., & Lv, P. (2018). Beekeeper: A blockchain-based iot system with secure storage and homomorphic computation. IEEE Access, 6, 43472–43488.

[14] Singh, S., Hosen, A. S., & Yoon, B. (2021). Blockchain security attacks, challenges, and solutions for the future distributed iot network. IEEE Access, 9, 13938–13959.

[15] Javaid, M., Haleem, A., Singh, R. P., Khan, S., & Suman, R. (2021). Blockchain technology applications for Industry 4.0: A literature-based review. Blockchain: Research and Applications, 100027.

[16] Le, T., & Mutka, M. W. (2018, June). Capchain: A privacy preserving access control framework based on blockchain for pervasive environments. In *2018 IEEE International Conference on Smart Computing (SMARTCOMP). Taormina, Sicily, Italy* (pp. 57–64). IEEE.

[17] Adams, C. (2020). A privacy-preserving Blockchain with fine-grained access control. Security and Privacy, 3(2), e97.

[18] Liang, X., Shetty, S., Tosh, D., Kamhoua, C., Kwiat, K., & Njilla, L. (2017, May). Provchain: A blockchain-based data provenance architecture in cloud environment with enhanced privacy and availability. In *2017 17th IEEE/ACM International Symposium on Cluster, Cloud and Grid Computing (CCGRID), IIS, Banglore, India* (pp. 468–477). IEEE.

[19] Das, M., Tao, X., & Cheng, J. C. (2021). BIM security: A critical review and recommendations using encryption strategy and blockchain. Automation in Construction, 126, 103682.

[20] Zyskind, G., & Nathan, O. (2015, May). Decentralizing privacy: Using blockchain to protect personal data. In *2015 IEEE Security and Privacy Workshops. San Jose, California* (pp. 180–184). IEEE.

[21] Idrees, S. M., Nowostawski, M., Jameel, R., & Mourya, A. K. (2021). Security aspects of blockchain technology intended for industrial applications. Electronics, 10(8), 951.

[22] Tosh, D. K., Shetty, S., Liang, X., Kamhoua, C. A., Kwiat, K. A., & Njilla, L. (2017, May). Security implications of blockchain cloud with analysis of block withholding attack. In *2017 17th IEEE/ACM International Symposium on Cluster, Cloud and Grid Computing (CCGRID. Taormina, Sicily, Italy)* (pp. 458–467). IEEE.

[23] Yuan, C., Xu, M. X., & Si, X. M. (2017). Research on a new signature scheme on blockchain. Security and Communication Networks, Hindawi.

[24] Sun, S. F., Au, M. H., Liu, J. K., & Yuen, T. H. (2017, September). Ringct 2.0: A compact accumulator-based (linkable ring signature) protocol for blockchain cryptocurrency monero. In *European Symposium on Research in Computer Security* (pp. 456–474). Springer, Cham.

[25] Narula, N., Vasquez, W., & Virza, M. (2018). {zkLedger}:{Privacy-Preserving} Auditing for Distributed Ledgers. In *15th USENIX Symposium on Networked Systems Design and Implementation (NSDI 18)*. RENTON, WA, USA (pp. 65–80).

[26] Pavithran, D., Al-Karaki, J. N., & Shaalan, K. (2021). Edge-based blockchain architecture for event-driven IoT using hierarchical identity based encryption. Information Processing & Management, 58(3), 102528.

[27] Dinh, T. T. A., Liu, R., Zhang, M., Chen, G., Ooi, B. C., & Wang, J. (2018). Untangling blockchain: A data processing view of blockchain systems. IEEE Transactions on Knowledge and Data Engineering, 30(7), 1366–1385.

Index